Classic Country Inns of America

The Mid-Atlantic and The South

CLASSIC COUNTRY INNS OF AMERICA
VOLUME 2

Inns of
The Mid-Atlantic
and
The South

BY PETER ANDREWS

PHOTOGRAPHED BY GEORGE W. GARDNER

AN ARCHITECTURAL DIGEST BOOK

THE KNAPP PRESS
LOS ANGELES

Copyright © 1978 by Knapp
Communications Corporation
Published in the United States of
America in 1978
The Knapp Press
5900 Wilshire Boulevard, Los
Angeles, California 90036
All rights reserved, including the
right to reproduce this book or
portions thereof in any form.
Trade edition distributed by Holt,
Rinehart and Winston in the
United States and simultaneously
by Holt, Rinehart and Winston of
Canada, Limited.

Library of Congress Cataloging in Publication Data

Andrews, Peter, 1931–
  Inns of the Mid-Atlantic and the South.

  (His Classic country inns of America; v. 2)
1. Hotels, taverns, etc.—Middle States. 2. Hotels,
taverns, etc.—Southern States. I. Gardner, George W.,
joint author. II. Title. III. Series.
TX909.A582   647'.9475   77-71352
ISBN 0-03-042841-6

First Edition
Printed in the United States of America
10 9 8 7 6 5 4 3 2 1

CONTENTS

* Photographed by Lilo Raymond

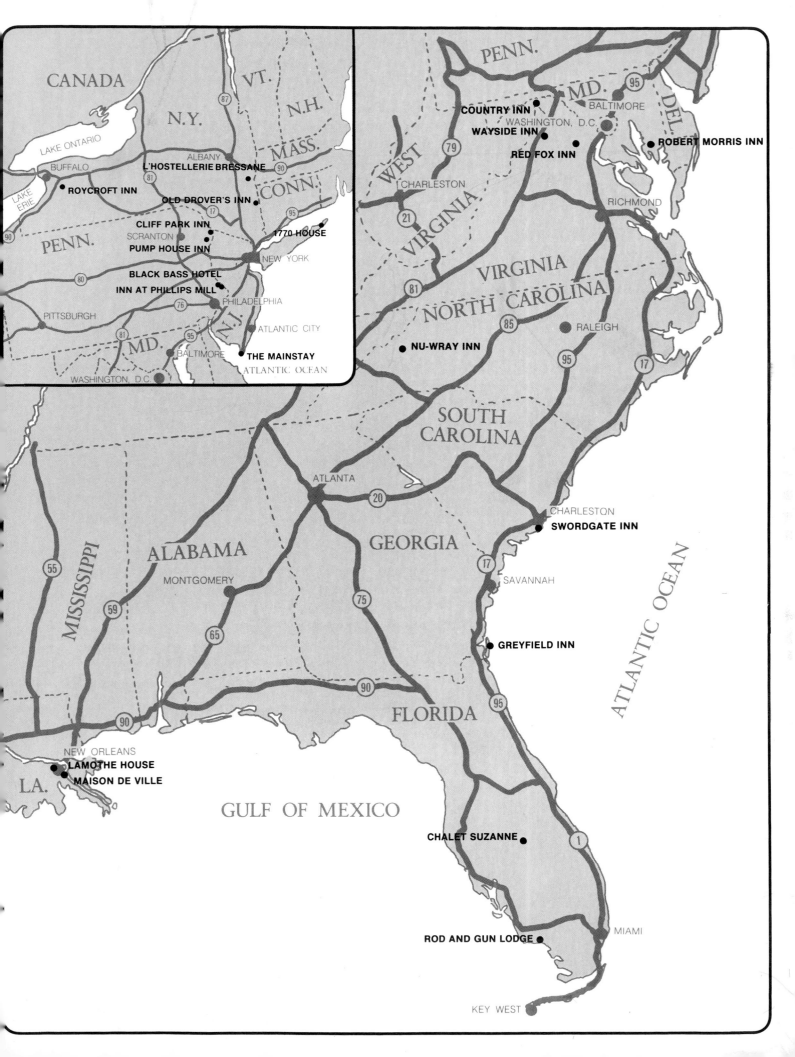

Kitty and Frank Turgeon
Roycroft Inn

THE REASSURANCE OF VARIETY

It takes the right amalgam of place, provender and personality to create a perfect country inn. The quirky, the individual, the unique are welcome, of course; if styles of innkeeping followed a predictable pattern, inns wouldn't be the delightful places they are. The stretch of country from upstate New York to Florida contains inns in great variety, and innkeepers, too. They are a confraternity of free spirits, united by their pursuit of a congenial ideal—the creation of a good place to be.

Carl and Vita Hinshaw run Chalet Suzanne, a gathering of imaginative pavilions in Lake Wales, Florida, that rambles over its tropic setting like the dream city of an exotic civilization. It could not be more different from the modest red brick house in upstate New York that Chef Jean Morel runs as L'Hostellerie Bressane. Yet both are fine restaurants, among the most celebrated in the nation, run by people whose hospitality tempts guests to return again and again.

Jean Morel's house is old—1782; Chalet Suzanne was built during the last forty years, but its spirit is a timeless one. There are places, though, that are the creation of time, tradition and good use. The Cliff Park Inn in Milford, Pennsylvania, was built as a farmhouse in 1820. It has been functioning as an inn since 1913, and the Buchanan family that runs it today ran it then. They are active, too, in the upkeep of the place, down to the youngest of the new generation. Thus in the spirit

Henri Drucquer
and Todd Drucquer
The Pump House

8

and activities of the inn there is a sense of tradition. Cliff Park is old, but lively, vigorous and changing.

Sometimes new innkeepers can impart new life to an old building. That's certainly true at the Red Fox Tavern in Middleburg, Virginia, a venerable Georgian pile whose slide to decrepitude was reversed by Nancy Brown Reuter, its new innkeeper, who invested a substantial amount to revive the inn's fortunes. She feels that the past must be revered with gusto—a sense of humor, style and occasion. The renewed Red Fox, long a gathering place for fox-hunting Virginians, has been returned to its habitués and is once again a center of community life.

Cape May, New Jersey, is an old resort town that never entered the twentieth century. It has been discovered by people seeking out what is now so rare in the United States, a coherent community—in Cape May's case, a community of Victorian seaside houses. The Mainstay in Cape May was a museum before Tom and Sue Carroll took over—and a darker, less scintillating example of the Victorian age could hardly be imagined. The Carrolls, like many young people with an interest in the past, have seen the old resort through new eyes. Today the interiors and exteriors of the Mainstay, which they now run as an inn, sparkle like the sea by which it sits, testimony to a lively recycling of the past. The delights of the present are not neglected, though. For Sue's carefully prepared breakfasts, Tom stays up late, readying the ingredients she needs, such as strawberries to go in the next morning's crêpes.

Extraordinary attention, long hours and devotion to guests' needs are characteristic of innkeepers. At an establishment like Maison de

LEFT
Ralph Chandler,
Janey Stibbs,
William Prentiss,
Kathleen Tingle
Maison de Ville

BELOW LEFT
Sidney and Miriam Perle
1770 *House*

BELOW
Rush Wray
Nu-Wray Inn

Kerry Anderson
Swordgate Inn

Ville in New Orleans, guests' needs are serviced with unusual completeness, for William Prentiss and his staff aim to outdo the finest of European hotels. Their care extends to placing a mint wrapped in foil on guests' pillows, a soothing token to top the indulgences that dining out in New Orleans can lead to.

Some inns, of course, plan indulgences of their own. At 1770 House, on Long Island in New York, innkeeper Miriam Perle is the chef and serves an eclectic and satisfying mixture of dishes from her experience with Italian, French and other cuisines. The menu is well suited to guests who, on a weekend's holiday from New York City, are likely to dine at East Hampton.

The 1770 has a perfect foil in the down-home hospitality of the Nu-Wray Inn, in Burnsville, North Carolina, where innkeepers Rush Wray and his sister Annie Wray Bennett make sure there are always enough homemade biscuits to sop up their delicious red-eye gravy.

Gertrude Munson
Lamothe House

There are also inns where a more ceremonious tone prevails. In this age of the offhand, it is sometimes a relief and a reassurance to encounter a bit of gracious formality. At the Lamothe House in New Orleans, innkeeper Gertrude Munson creates an atmosphere of Old World civility. Ceremonies of a slightly different sort, the careful rituals of sport fishing, surround guests at the spare yet luxurious Rod and Gun Lodge in Everglades City, Florida. Innkeeper Martin Bowen honors the tradition of the sportsmen's club that the inn once was.

Formal, club-like, down-home or worldly wise, the inns in this book demonstrate the enormous diversity of a thriving American institution. Their charms are those of their creators, innkeepers whose devotion to other people's comfort and satisfaction make them at once host, actor, confidant, sometime chef and tour guide. In an age of specialization, they bring back a sense of wholeness to the American scene.

Tom and Sue Carroll
Mainstay Inn

12

OLD DROVERS INN

Dover Plains, New York

The inn's original owners were a pair of worthy Quaker brothers, John and Ebenezer Preston, who built the Clear Water Tavern over a natural spring in 1750. Apparently they had hoped to run an abstemious establishment that would not sell any liquor; but tavern keeping in the eighteenth century was a tough business, and the Preston brothers had to bend with the times to keep their customers. The Marquis de Lafayette caused a minor scandal when he arrived from France in 1777 and appeared at the inn in the company of a horde of "fancy ladies." But the real problem came from the tavern's regulars, a group of rough-and-tumble drovers from New England who bought herds of cattle and swine up north and drove them down the post roads for sale in New York. It was thirsty work, and the men expected something more than clear water when they stopped at the tavern. The Preston brothers compromised; instead of actually selling their customers drinks, they put a barrel of rum in front of the fireplace with a sign saying, "Drink what ye will. Pay what ye may." It proved to be a happy arrangement, and the inn prospered mightily.

More than two hundred years later, the inn is still catering to its clientele with flawless service and huge cocktails in fifteen-ounce glasses. Bought in 1937 by Olin Chester Potter, and renamed the Old Drovers Inn, this small but roomy establishment has become one of the best-known country inns in America. Still in the Potter family, it is managed by innkeeper Travis Harris, who has been here for more than thirty years. "I grew up with the inn," Travis relates. "In all that time, there haven't been many changes. We've kept it pretty much the way it's always been."

There isn't very much you'd want to change at the Drovers Inn. In

Worth the drive.

Located only seventy-five miles from New York City, the Old Drovers is one of America's best-known inns. The Meeting Room, above, so called because it was formerly used for town meetings, is the inn's most popular bedroom.

The Taproom.

Heavy beams, low ceilings and hand-etched hurricane lamps make the Taproom, left, an intimate setting for drinks and dinner. The Old Drovers is well known for its fine food. The hand-lettered menu outside the Taproom gives an idea of the fare.

terms of service, décor and ambiance, it has always been a classic country inn. The good service begins the moment guests arrive. Their luggage is whisked upstairs, and in winter the fire is lit in their bedroom before they have a chance to wend their way up the succession of stairways leading to the upper floors. One bedroom features a comfortable mahogany sleigh bed, and all the rooms have a puffy down quilt folded at the foot of each bed. The Federal Room, which serves as the breakfast room for overnight guests and is also sometimes used for private parties, is decorated in the Federal style with six smooth, mahogany tables, each with its own brightly polished Georgian candelabrum. Breakfast at the inn is a special treat, offering sausage specially ground for the inn in New York, served with stacks of blueberry griddle cakes, and steaming hot coffee from an antique silver coffee pot.

The most popular bedroom upstairs is the Meeting Room, a spectacular, twenty-by-twenty-foot, sunny yellow bedroom with a high, vaulted barrel ceiling. Down a flight of stairs is a small library with an extensive collection of nineteenth-century English novels.

The most historic area of all is the Taproom downstairs, a dining room and bar with a huge, seventeen-by-seventeen-foot chimney that holds the building together structurally. This is appropriate, because it is the restaurant that has given the Old Drovers its reputation.

One restaurant critic said that the inn was the 21 Club of out-of-town eating places. As with that famous New York City restaurant, the inn is a cavern of dark, gleaming wood paneling and is filled with a wealth of art objects and period paintings.

The service is attentive. A waiter brings a blackboard with the evening's menu, which he clips to the low beamed ceiling by the table for diners to make their choices. Cheddar soup is a splendid house specialty, along with shrimp rarebit and stuffed partridge—the game fowl are raised for the inn on a nearby farm. For dessert, guests may choose either something light, such as a delicate raspberry sherbet with Cassis or lose all discretion and order a marvelously rich apple cheesecake topped with walnuts and coconut. Either way, dining at the Old Drovers Inn is a unique experience, and the little touches never seem to end. Even before the meal begins, cocktails are served with a complimentary platter of deviled eggs sprinkled with dark brown, hickory-smoked salt. Travis Harris estimates that in his time at the inn he has served eight million deviled eggs. But at the Old Drovers Inn, who's counting?

18

The Federal Room.

The public rooms are generally large, dark and comfortable. The Federal Room, used for breakfast and private parties, is decorated with a mural painted by Edward Paine in 1941.

The library

provides a tranquil setting for reading, conversation or quiet reflection.

L'HOSTELLERIE BRESSANE

Hillsdale, New York

Monsieur
le chef.

Jean Morel, inset, has
turned an unassuming,
two-hundred-year-old,
rural house in New York
State into one of America's
finest restaurants. In 1978
he was named a Master
Chef of France by
l'Association des maîtres
cuisinier de France. One of
his vegetable specialties is
eggplant Provencal, seen
above in preparation.

The entries in the guest book tell the story. When
members of the Boston Symphony dined at L'Hostellerie Bressane, they wrote, "We're proud to taste the
symphonies of a great artist."

Robert Redford ate there and had one cautionary
note: "Please," the actor implored, "don't expand."
It was the kind of plea that people make when they
have discovered a perfect spot and don't want anything
to change. L'Hostellerie Bressane is just such a place—an impeccable
French restaurant and inn located in the heart of New York's rural
Columbia County.

The proprietor-chef and chief miracle worker of the establishment
is Jean Morel, a master of haute cuisine with an impressive set of
credentials. Schooled in his native France, he was chef at the Château-
briand in New York City, and later at the Lafayette in the days when
it seemed that Jacqueline Kennedy didn't know any other restaurant
in the city. Chef Morel grew tired of urban life and began to look
around for a place in the country. He found a somewhat square, brick
structure in Hillsdale that seemed just right.

Built in 1782, the place did not have a particularly distinguished
history. Shortly after the Revolutionary War, this Dutch Colonial coach
stop was used as the Hillsdale town jail. But it had many of the essential
elements that make a building ripe for restoration: wide plank flooring,
graceful Palladian windows, a plenitude of strong antique brick and
no less than eight fireplaces with their original colonial mantels. In
1971, Chef Morel bought the place and opened for business as the
Dutch Hearth Inn.

The *Albany Times Union* came to Chef Morel's table and decreed
it to be the restaurant against which all others in the area must

As the maitre d' selects a bottle of wine, and then serves a perfect rack of lamb done to a succulent pink, Chef Morel, above, slices the delicate smoked salmon appetizer.

henceforth be judged. The *New York Times* made the journey north and gave it three stars; the *Mobil Guide* gave four. Suddenly, this quiet byway in the farm country of upstate New York had a restaurant on a par with the finest in the country.

Chef Morel was master of the Dutch Hearth for five years. In 1977, however, he changed its name to L'Hostellerie Bressane in honor of his native region of Bresse, an area of France with a rich culinary tradition. People who come to enjoy the hospitality of Jean and his wife, Madeleine, find a delightful combination of an Early American inn sparkling with the atmosphere of a Lyon *hostellerie*. The Morels have furnished the inn with their own family heirlooms and unusual antiques from the Netherlands. Colorful Delft tiles surround one of the hearths, while upstairs are four cozy bedrooms, each with its own fireplace. The rooms are charming and comfortable, but their chief appeal is that they are not far from the dining room. Often, guests book a room on the busy weekends just to be sure they will have a reservation for dinner.

The care that Chef Morel takes is obvious in every phase of the dining experience at L'Hostellerie. "In our little hotel," he says, mixing a white crème de menthe with Perrier, "everything must be first class." And so it is, from the extensive wine cellar, which features vintages as dear as $120 a bottle, to the classic antique Windsor chairs and the tables always set with fresh flowers.

A restaurant-business adage holds that no matter how attractive the setting, everything begins in the kitchen. As with all great chefs, Jean Morel knows everything begins even before that. Good dining begins with the ingredients. Chef Morel is up before dawn to personally select the vegetables and fresh produce for the day. The meats are driven up daily from New York City, and the turbot is flown in from France. "There are no shortcuts in a first-class restaurant," Chef Morel insists, and every sauce, every soup stock and every pastry crust is created from scratch. There is no skimping, either. No cooking wines are used at L'Hostellerie Bressane. All the wines, even the champagne for the sauces, are a premium grade.

Even in the finest kitchen, there is a danger of stagnation or of repeating the same successful dishes over and over again until the touch becomes mechanical. In order to keep up with the latest developments

22

in French cuisine, Jean and Madeleine close for almost two months in the early part of each year to return to France.

All their effort and care pay off each night at dinner. The menu of L'Hostellerie Bressane is a marvel. Even the most traditional dish is served with a special Jean Morel flair. "Everyone has onion soup," he says, pointing to the menu, "but no one adds egg yolks, Madeira and Cognac." Few chefs do many things the way Jean Morel does. Soufflé of chicken livers in cream, fresh artichoke hearts with paté de foie gras and truffles, broiled baby lobster in garlic butter and braised sweetbreads with chestnuts and Port are only a few of the unmatched specialties of the house.

Chef Morel's fame is so widespread that he also runs an occasional four-day cooking seminar for students who come to the inn to learn from him.

"Taste," the master says, "taste, taste and taste. You must taste the food. You read in books that something must simmer for half an hour. That is nonsense. You must taste it. That will tell you when it is ready. Taste is everything."

Grande maison.

The priorities at L'Hostellerie Bressane are unambiguous. There are as many dining rooms as there are bedrooms. At the left the waiter is cautiously serving a dessert soufflé, while below another dessert is being prepared in the kitchen. The bar is a special place where a French breakfast of croissants and coffee is served in the morning sunshine.

A
proper
front.
Except for the addition of
an entranceway, the
symmetrical façade of the
house retains its original
colonial appearance.

1770 HOUSE

East Hampton, Long Island, New York

The 1770 House is a trim, white-shingled restaurant and inn on the main street of East Hampton, a community that has often been called "the most beautiful village in America." Guests at the old Long Island inn would find it hard to deny the claim. The original town hall, a simple one-room structure built in 1731, still stands next door and next to it is the old Clinton Academy, once the oldest academic institution in the state. Today this handsome building, with its porches and cupola, houses the Clinton Museum. Down the street is a cluster of old buildings that are showplaces of early Long Island country construction, including a windmill, and the house that was the "Home Sweet Home" John Howard Payne wrote about in 1823.

In the past twenty years, before its present renovation, the 1770 House had become a somewhat shabby element among all this spruce early architecture. During its long life, the building had been used as a general store, a private home, a dining hall for the students at Clinton Academy, a boarding house and a public inn. During the 1940s and early '50s, it had been an engaging spot, popular with the show business celebrities appearing at the historic John Drew Theater across the street. Many actors, including Clark Gable, were guests. But by the late 1960s, the charming old place had been largely uncared for by a series of owners and fell into disarray and ill repair.

As so often happens, the place was saved by an energetic couple who wanted to start a new life for themselves in an old house. Sidney Perle was a successful sportswear shop owner and his wife, Miriam, ran her own cooking school and catering service. They decided to go into semiretirement and looked around for a small country inn to buy and run themselves. The first fact they discovered is that there is nothing

Brass
bound.
Innkeeper Sidney Perle has
set up the elements of an
old teller's cage to mark
off his office from the rest
of the sun porch. His
fondness for brass is
evident in many gleaming
appurtenances of the inn.

28

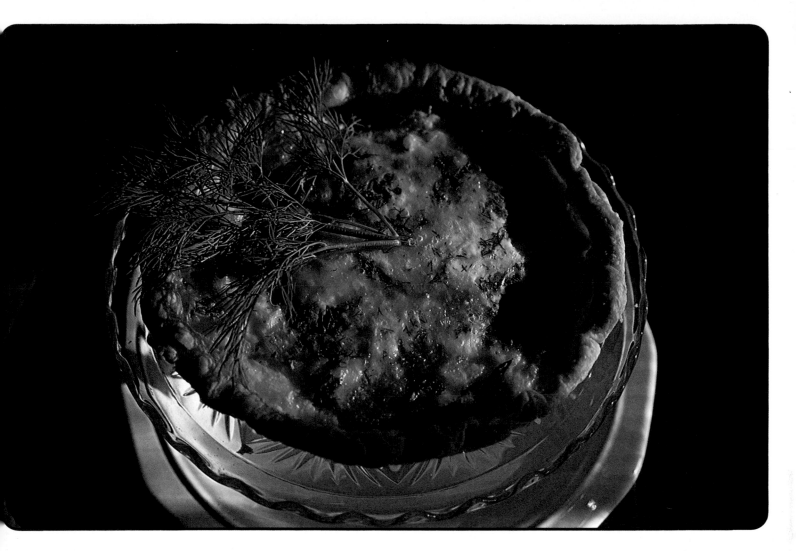

Set for satisfaction.

The restaurant's bamboo-patterned chairs are Regency in design, as is the chandelier. It could be from a pavilion visited by Beau Brummell, but the Perles think it probably came from a nightclub. The 1770's menu changes weekly. On one night guests might begin with Miriam's fabulous quiche, above, or poached salmon with sour cream and dill sauce, then perhaps soup Pistou, move on to rack of lamb persilée with fresh, minted pears and finish with the inn's famous whiskey cake.

"retiring" about being innkeepers, especially when they find and fall in love with a beat-up relic of the eighteenth century.

"The place was a wreck," Sid recalls. "It had been stripped bare. Even the old doorknobs were gone. The last owners just walked away from the place and let it go. There were more than two hundred burst pipes, and half a foot of water in the basement. But it was basically such a fine old house, we couldn't resist it."

They bought the ramshackle structure and spent months scraping, painting, plugging and generally putting the place in order. Now, thanks to their work, the 1770 House can once again take its rightful place among its distinguished neighbors.

Outside, the house has been restored to its original, spanking white; inside, the refurbished rooms serve as a setting for the Perles' extensive collection of mid- to late-nineteenth-century antiques.

The Perles have brought a light, modern touch to their renovation. On one wall, there is a charming portrait of Miriam's mother, and next to it hangs a colonial portrait Miriam painted from a model in a book. "I needed a colonial ancestor for the place," she explains, "so I painted one of my own."

Both the Perles are members of the American Clock Society, and their collection of period timepieces is worth a visit in itself. All the clocks in the house still work, even though they do not always agree on exactly what time it is. The dining room is a striking combination of old and new decorative flourishes. The walls are a deep chocolate brown, but

A
corner
table
in the dining room, backed
by a Rogers group of Faust
and Marguerite and a
stained-glass panel
depicting a pre-Raphaelite
maiden.

On a
figured
ground.
Miriam's flair for bright
and vigorous design shows
throughout the inn. It is
evident in the stained-glass
panel hung near the bay
window in the dining
room, the patterned shade
on the sun porch, a
composition including the
carved face from a
carousel and the Italian
figurine in the window.

the room appears light and airy because all the wooden trim has been
painted white. Each table is highlighted with an old shaving mug filled
with fresh flowers.

The inn has six comfortable bedrooms upstairs, each with its own
bath. "One of the many owners of this place was a plumber," says
Miriam, "so we have plenty of bathrooms."

Her special preserve is the kitchen, a spacious room that rises clear
to the rafters, where she conducts a cooking school in addition to
preparing the regular meals for the restaurant. The food at 1770 House
is what Miriam, a Cordon Bleu graduate, calls "the Cuisine of Today,"
an eclectic mixture of tastes and styles from many different countries.
Among the hors d'oeuvres and desserts are such intriguing dishes as
puffed crêpes and honey butter, blintzes Florentine, *vacherin* Cassis
and apple brown betty topped with marzipan. The colonial taproom

The afternoon sun shines through the curtained window of a back bedroom.

Staying power.

A warm fire on the eighteenth-century hearth in the downstairs taproom encourages guests to linger. The enameled tin plates on the mantel are from another of the Perles' collections: early advertising art.

33

A note of color.

Each of the six bedrooms at 1770 has a distinctive, dominant color—brown in this front bedroom overlooking East Hampton's Main Street.

is used year-round for predinner and post-theater refreshments, with the emphasis on homemade desserts. The Perles' daughter Wendy is the pastry chef, and son Adam works behind the bar.

Restoring an old inn is an adventure full of surprises, as anyone can attest who has ever taken out what appeared to be a nonbearing wall only to find the ceiling above collapsing. The surprises are not always pleasant. So far, however, Sid and Miriam have been lucky. They had assumed the house was built in 1770, but internal evidence, as adjudged from the beehive oven in the cellar fireplace, may place the main part of the house in the 1730s, making it one of the oldest homes in town. They began to strip down one of the walls in the library, not sure what they would find underneath the two centuries of repeated enamelings. After more than a month of solid work, they uncovered a marvelous example of delicately patterned tombstone paneling in soft pecan. Traditionally, this kind of woodwork was painted over in the eighteenth century, but the Perles have decided to leave it as is, a gently glowing reminder of the unexpected pleasures of innkeeping.

Little journey to East Aurora,

home of Elbert Hubbard, writer, philosopher, orator, publisher. The Roycroft Inn, which he owned and managed, was the hub of his arts and crafts revival. Today it is the center of a new arts movement.

ROYCROFT INN

East Aurora, New York

Alice's office.

Formerly Mrs. Hubbard's office, the room at left is now used for banquets. Innkeeper Kitty Turgeon has assembled a diverse collection of art honoring the American Indian, whose civilization was one of Hubbard's deep concerns.

"There is no failure except in no longer trying" was the personal maxim of Elbert Hubbard. One of the most extraordinary men in modern American history, Hubbard devoted a lifetime to proving the truth of his own adage.

He was a great coiner of maxims. Whenever one sees an inspirational message framed on someone's office wall, there is a very good chance that Elbert Hubbard said it first. At the turn of the century, his exhortations on behalf of the Protestant work ethic were found in almost every shop, office and factory in America.

Hubbard did more than invent maxims. He lived them. "Work to become, not just acquire" was another of his favorites, and Hubbard became many men during his active life. As an executive with the Larkin Soap Company, he was one of the pioneers in developing sophisticated mass-marketing techniques. After a successful career in the business world, Hubbard became a writer. When editors were reluctant to publish his writings, he started his own magazine.

In 1894, following the model of William Morris in England, Hubbard established an independent guild of craftsmen, known as the Roycrofters, to create fine books and practice other crafts. The complex was as self-contained as Hubbard could make it, but he bristled when it was called a commune. Its members were paid wages and lived in their own homes in and around East Aurora.

Hubbard was a restless soul. In 1915, when he was almost sixty years old, he set off for Europe to report on trench warfare in France during World War I. He never got there; Hubbard and his second wife perished in the sinking of the *Lusitania*.

A man for all seasons.

Elbert Hubbard's idols included Voltaire, Kant, and Marcus Aurelius. His *Little Journeys,* a series of volumes written to acquaint the newly literate population with Western culture, stands atop an oaken desk in the Ruskin Room.

Hubbard was once accused of being a fraud, but one of his adages was, "What others say of me matters little, what I myself say and do matters much." He espoused several then unpopular causes, ranging from taxation of church property to women's rights. His turbulent private life included involvement in a scandalous divorce action, a situation that disturbed his many dedicated followers. Hubbard had an adage for that as well: "Never explain: Your friends do not need it, and your enemies will not believe you anyway."

The stained glass was
made by Dart Hunter, one
of the original Roycroft
artists.

38

The Ruskin Room.

*"Life without industry
is guilt, industry with-
out art is brutality."*
JOHN RUSKIN

Hubbard admired John
Ruskin, the English social
philosopher and art critic,
whose ideas seemed to
dovetail with his own. The
Ruskin Room, photos right
and lower left, is an
informal museum of
Hubbard's life and
includes many of his
books, hand-illuminated
manuscripts, ornate
bookbindings and pottery.

His son Elbert Hubbard II kept the Roycroft shops going until they
failed in 1938, belated victims of the Great Depression. For several
years, Roycroft was little more than a boarding house, until it was
purchased by Frank Turgeon.

The inn has been restored by Frank's wife, Kitty, in consultation
with members of the Hubbard family. Together they revitalized the old
house in a way that Elbert certainly would have appreciated. It is at
once imposing and quietly comfortable. The front door is carved,
naturally enough, with an Elbert Hubbard maxim: "Produce Great
People—The Rest Follows."

The main rooms in the inn are named after men and events that were
important in Hubbard's life. The Ali Baba Bar is named for Anson
Blackman, a close associate; Ali Baba was his name within the
Roycrofters. It is now a modern discotheque, but the ambiance still
recalls the times when Hubbard, with his long hair and flowing artist's
bow tie, would come to the inn and fire the gathered craftsmen with
his inspirational oratory.

The old permanent apartments upstairs are being converted into bedrooms, with walls covered in burlap and blinds made of matchstick bamboo. Kitty Turgeon has carefully searched Hubbard's original writings to ensure the accuracy of her restoration.

A group of craftsmen called Roycrofters-at-Large now occupy most of the original complex. Under the direction of Nancy Hubbard Brady, Elbert's granddaughter, they strive to maintain the same high standards of craftsmanship the original group had. There are several working studios where visitors can see how traditional crafts are practiced today: an antique printing press, a pottery studio, a jeweler's workshop and a handweaver's workshop. Elbert Hubbard would doubtless be delighted with all of this activity. New generations are able to learn about old crafts and to see how much beauty a single person can create with only a few tools and a boundless imagination. Once again, Roycroft is "devoted to the business of living."

40

The mark of excellence.

This unique and exciting gift shop offers a dazzling array of handcrafted Roycroft items. The high standards of Hubbard's day prevail. A jury of members judges each design before it can be marked with the intertwining RR, for Roycroft Revival, and offered for sale.

The Larkin Room,

the inn's most popular dining area, is named for the Larkin Soap Company, where Hubbard, as sales manager, acquired his original fame and fortune.

Levis Falls House, Canadensis, Pa.

PUMP HOUSE INN

Canadensis, Pennsylvania

Innkeeping par excellence since 1842.

One of the first inns in the Poconos, the Pump House today is widely known for its excellent French cuisine. The building now looks much the same as it always did. Above it is shown in an early photograph, when it was named the Leavis Falls House.

"Our first idea was to be an inn with a small restaurant attached to it," explains innkeeper Todd Drucquer. "But somehow it all got turned around. Our family is originally from France, and good food is an important part of our heritage. So now we have a first-class restaurant with four overnight guest rooms upstairs."

Either way, the little town of Canadensis is all the richer for three generations of the Drucquer family, who moved here in 1965 and opened the Pump House Inn. The inn, a perky little cream-colored shingled building with bright red colonial shutters, sits on a hillside in the heart of the Pocono Mountains resort country. It is very much a family-run establishment. In the evenings, Todd and his father, Henri, are on hand to greet guests as they arrive. On the weekends, Todd's two young sons are likely to be playing in the front room. The main floors of the Pump House are filled with unusual family touches. The taproom contains a delightful collection of model ships and nautical paintings from the days when Henri's father was a prominent shipbuilder. The much-traveled Drucquer family has a particular affinity for South America, and they have decorated the inn with several interesting examples of Latin crafts. While digging the foundation for a new dining room, they uncovered a thirty-five-ton rock that they were unable to budge. So they left it where it was, used it for a waterfall, and built the dining room around it.

Both Henri and Todd were executives for large international corporations before moving to Canadensis, so they know how much weary travelers appreciate modern conveniences. The four bedrooms upstairs, each with its own bath, are pleasant, attractively decorated with large, comfortable beds, and excellently lit for reading.

While most of the guests spend their days enjoying the sporting facilities of the Pocono area, the inn seems to sleep the afternoon away. Actually, the kitchen, which is the heart and soul of the house, is busily preparing the evening meal. The Pump House Inn is famous for its food and has drawn rave reviews from restaurant critics all over America. Even more impressive than clippings, however, is the fact that many of the diners stay at one of the other nearby resorts and eat at the Pump House even though they must also pay for their meals at their own hotel.

The young and energetic chef, Mark Kaplan, operates a truly remarkable French kitchen that serves up the broadest possible range of Continental specialties. Depending on the night, there are three styles of dining available at the Pump House Inn. The bistro dinners recall the hearty peasant cooking of provincial France. These are typical country meals built around a single entrée, such as cassoulet or veal Marengo, and are served family style. The à la carte dinners are more elegant, and a typical evening's offerings might include a delicate paté with Cognac sauce, mushrooms stuffed with lobster and crabmeat, rack of lamb and poached salmon. One of the unusual specialties of the house is a Peruvian *seviche,* in which small bay scallops are not cooked

Wine lovers' paradise.

Innkeepers Henri Drucquer and son Todd have imported a selection of more than 1,400 wines, many from France, the original home of Henri's parents. These are two of the dining areas, where the wine collection is much in evidence.

The best way

for guests to dine at the Pump House is to reserve one of the charming rooms, check in early, dress unhurriedly, and then proceed expectantly to a waiting table in the dining room. Three hours later guests may then reverse the process, grateful for a comfortable bed after a memorable meal.

46

Family elegance.

Many of the antiques are from the home of Henri Drucquer, who assembled them on his travels. In the breakfast room at left there are several family portraits, this one being of the late Mrs. Henri Drucquer.

at all but are marinated for three days. On Thursday nights during the winter season, Chef Kaplan takes French cuisine about as far as it can go, in a series of culinary spectaculars. These special dinners are planned a week in advance, and reservations are mandatory. The menu at one recent feast started with a special creation of his in honor of the legendary French chef, Paul Bocuse: escargots, sautéed in Pernod butter, served *en croûte* with a combination of Mornay and Bordelaise sauces. Then followed in dizzying order: a smoked trout mousse; honey sherbet; a consommé with black mushrooms; lobster and sole quenelles; lime sherbet; roast pheasant with sausage, chestnuts, wild rice and apples in Calvados; fresh vegetable salad; and, finally, praline soufflé.

Here is a country inn with a fine personal touch, comfortable rooms and a kitchen that cooks, as one critic said, "as if God were watching."

BLACK BASS HOTEL
Lumberville, Pennsylvania

When Charles Dickens first came to America in 1842, he was not much taken with what he found. He did not care for our clothing, our speech or our manners. One of the few things that seemed to intrigue him was the sight of a horse-drawn boat working its way up and down the Delaware Canal. "A barge with a little house on it," was the way he described it. The accommodations aboard those nineteenth-century vessels were something less than first class. They usually handled about thirty passengers in spartan simplicity. There was a red drapery separating the ladies' quarters from the gentlemen's. Passengers of both sexes slept on narrow bunks that were little more than glorified bookshelves stacked up on either side of the cabin. Bathing facilities, should anyone care to utilize them, consisted of a dipper on a chain to scoop up canal water and a tin basin to stand in. Still, there were some amenities. There was a barber on board to shave the gentlemen; he also waited on table during the afternoon meal. The food was hearty, if undistinguished, and there was always plenty of whiskey, gin, brandy and rum in the ship's locker.

The real treat, however, came when the boat tied up at one of the many hotel facilities along the canal, where weary travelers were offered good food, a convivial taproom and a hot bath.

The Black Bass Hotel has been one of the favorite stopovers along the Delaware Canal for almost 250 years. It was built sometime during the 1740s to provide colonial travelers with a safe haven to spend the night in territory prowled by none-too-friendly Indians. Apparently the place was well fortified, because it carried on without incident for some ninety years. When trouble finally did come to the Black Bass, it was caused not by outside marauders but by the customers in the bar.

Tuned to the river's flow.

There has been an inn at this spot on the Delaware, just north of New Hope, for over two hundred years. The Black Bass combines artifacts from colonial America and the ante-bellum South with elegant decorative touches from Europe. The pewter pots shown above are from the inn's collection. *Overleaf,* the hotel at night seen from across the road.

Dining on the Delaware,

enjoying the splendid view and the inn's good food, dissolves the mundane cares of life. The open gallery is bordered with cast iron in a graceful grapevine pattern.

53

The royal touch

is seen in the bar, where the inn's extensive collection of British royal memorabilia contrasts with the varied collection of country chairs.

According to local legend, a group of canal men stopped by the Black Bass in the winter of 1832 and proceeded to make so merry that they came very close to blowing the establishment off the face of the earth. Somehow a fire broke out, but the hotel was saved when Major Anthony Fry rushed through the flames, broke into the cellar where the canal company stored a supply of blasting powder and carried it away before it blew the building sky-high. Even then, the Black Bass had a very loyal clientele.

Since 1949, the Black Bass Hotel has been the property and passion of Herb Ward. Herb is something of a character in a part of the country where characters are the rule rather than the exception. A few miles away, he is building another home, which he plans to heat entirely with wood and the sun's rays. Whether he is retreating to the nineteenth century or just getting ready for the twenty-first is hard to determine, but the twentieth century seems to hold little interest for him. Certainly the style and ambiance of the Black Bass Hotel evoke a time other than the present.

When the day begins at the Black Bass, the scene is pure Renoir as the misty veil of morning fog rolls in over the surging Delaware River. Most of the overnight guests have box seats for this morning show, as they have coffee on their private balconies.

The most elegant of the upstairs accommodations is a two-bedroom suite, with a private bath and living room. The rest have their own washstands but share two baths. Each bedroom is charmingly distinctive. One of the favorites is called "Le Bastard" [*sic*], supposedly named for its cast-off furniture, although why anyone would want to throw away a four-poster mahogany bed with a hand-crocheted bedspread and a handsome, marble-topped bureau is a mystery. The other rooms have their own flourishes, such as canopied beds or floor-to-ceiling headboards set off with antique quilts.

Herb Ward says he wants his guests to feel as if they're in the country, which is exactly where they are. But the question is, which part of the country? With its heavy, functional furniture and the spirit of Abraham Lincoln in one of the upstairs bedrooms, it could be Springfield, Illinois. The harpsicord in the downstairs lobby recalls the genteel country musicales of Braintree, Massachusetts. The wrought-iron balustrades on the upstairs balconies seem to have come straight from the Mississippi bayou country. Herb bristles at that thought, by the way. He claims that wrought iron was originally made in Pennsylvania and then shipped South, where its use became celebrated in New Orleans. Actually, where the guests really are is in Black Bass Hotel country, and there's no other region quite like it.

The downstairs rooms are large enough to handle the heavy dinner traffic and yet still manage to seem cozy and comfortable. The parlor is a good place to sit in one of the wing chairs in front of the fire and read the paper in the morning or to have a cocktail in the evening. All of the dining rooms have sweeping views of the Delaware River. The Wine Cellar Bar, which is almost on the water's edge, is now reserved for special parties and receptions. In furnishing the main downstairs rooms, Herb Ward has combined the best elements of an English pub and a colonial tavern. The tables are old animal slaughtering benches lacquered to a high gloss. The decorations on the wall have a heavy English flavor. Something of a royalist at heart, Herb has amassed a

huge collection of memorabilia about the British royal family. He has commemorative plates, and other artifacts, from the reigns of every British monarch since Victoria, who is shown in royal procession on the splendid diorama at the back of the bar.

The Black Bass dining room offers an extensive menu, with heavy emphasis on traditional American and English dishes. Cold cucumber soup, Meeting Street crab with cream sauce, roast duck and Benjamin Franklin's smoked oysters are typical items on the menu.

In the evenings, particularly on weekends during the summer season, the Black Bass is not exactly a quiet, sleepy, little roadside tavern. The dining rooms are usually filled, and there is a piano player in the bar who apparently knows the score of every Broadway musical comedy since *The Black Crook*. Singing is encouraged after dinner, and the pewter-topped bar, which was once at Maxim's in Paris, is one of the most popular spots along the river.

Mr. Ward's private collection.

Herb Ward, owner of the Black Bass, has been buying and selling antiques all his life. The beds shown here, including the one in Le Bastard room, upper left, are some of his prize finds.

In the mornings, however, the hotel once again becomes the peaceful waystop it has been for two-and-a-half centuries. There is a clutch of interesting shops across from the hotel and several historic sights in the area. The river is also a delightful attraction. A favorite diversion of Black Bass guests is to go to the general store a few yards down the road to buy some cheese and a loaf of the magnificent locally produced black bread and picnic along the Delaware.

The Black Bass Hotel has one final distinction unusual for this part of the country. People in this historic area are apt to put up a plaque proclaiming "George Washington Slept Here" on no more evidence than the possibility that the general's horse might have stopped to have a drink somewhere in the area. There is no such plaque at the Black Bass. As Herb is fond of pointing out, throughout the long and desperate travail of the American Revolution, the Black Bass Hotel stood resolutely loyal to the Crown and wouldn't let Washington have even a tot of rum, much less a room for the night.

Keys to the animal kingdom.
The hotel has always had a favorite pet in residence. Puss and Rabbit are two from the past who are buried in the tiny graveyard near the inn.

Crack of dawn.
The early morning mist rising over the Delaware is an unforgettable sight. In the distance is a footbridge which crosses the river just above the inn.

THE INN
AT PHILLIPS MILL

New Hope, Pennsylvania

At the sign of the copper pig.

The sign at left recalls the fact that the inn once adjoined a piggery. It still has a rural environment; animal sounds from a nearby farm occasionally break the country stillness. The wild flowers, above, are dried and arranged by a local horticulturalist.

Entering the Inn at Phillips Mill, it's hard to believe that this snug, stone inn on the Delaware River has not been receiving guests for at least a century or so. Everything seems exactly suited for gracious innkeeping. But the cheery little porker cut out of copper hanging over the front door commemorates the fact that, when built in 1750, the building served as a barn next to the piggery of one of the great pre-Revolutionary estates in Bucks County. In the 1800s it was an artist's studio and then part of the Holmquist School for Girls. Its transformation to an inn came about only in 1973, when architect Brooks Kaufman and his wife, Joyce, took it over.

Brooks handled the structural restoration, and Joyce was responsible for the interior design. People who say their houses are too small to do anything with should journey to the inn just to see what taste and imagination can accomplish, even in the smallest places. The inn is tiny: there are only five bedrooms upstairs; a sitting room, a small dining room and an enclosed porch are downstairs. And yet the house contains every amenity one would expect to find in an establishment five times its size. The inn is filled with a series of small but deft effects. The lounge area consists of a large couch in front of a walk-in fireplace in the sitting room; one may dine there completely unobtrusive to other guests. In one of the upstairs bedrooms, which is too small to accommodate a traditional canopied bed, Joyce has covered the room with a charming fabric so that the entire ceiling appears to be a canopy. A tiny three-by-six-foot bath has been transformed into a picturebook room, painted in bright pumpkin and lined with mirrors. Even the

Sophisticated Bucks County

diners welcome the food at Phillips Mill. A variety of especially well-prepared vegetables complement each dish, including the tournedos, above. Guests may dine in front of the fireplace or upstairs, where a private dining room assures quiet and a homelike atmosphere.

61

Pennsylvania pastoral.

The Delaware River Canal, left, is a short walk from the inn's front door. Serenity reigns today where towlines pulled barges in the past.

exposed radiators have been made into slender, white grace notes. In less skillful hands it could have been close quarters; instead, the inn is delightfully intimate.

Situated in the heart of some of the most historically significant countryside in America, the inn fairly echoes the past. It was near here, in the desperate shank end of 1776, when the Revolution seemed to have ended almost before it had begun, that George Washington, at the head of a retreating, shoeless army, remarked to one of his officers, "I think the game is pretty near up." Many of the historic sites of those terrible times have been preserved as national landmarks: Summerseat, where Washington made his headquarters; the church in Allentown, where the Continentals hid the Liberty Bell to keep it out of British hands; and the Thompson-Neely House, where Washington's

Très intime.

Guests ascend the narrow stairs to a room in the inn's private world of comfort. Each morning, a basket with all the ingredients for *petit déjeuner* is placed outside guests' doors. In the bath, above, almond soap is provided.

officers helped plan the reckless Christmas Night scramble over the Delaware River for the attack on Trenton that saved the Revolution. All are within easy reach of the inn.

Whatever the day's activity—visiting the historic sites of the Revolution, a bit of antiquing in the literally hundreds of shops in the area or just taking a leisurely trip along the old Delaware Canal—guests at the inn usually make sure they are back by dinner. The kitchen at Phillips Mill is one of the most skillful in the area.

One benefit of the inn's intimacy is that even on the busiest evening in the summer season, chef Dominique Ponton can match the cuisine served in the finest New York City restaurants. The menu tends toward the Continental, and the specialties of the house, such as tournedos Henry IV with artichoke hearts and Béarnaise sauce, are served with a flourish. Attention to the most minute detail is the hallmark of the kitchen. A simple dish of carrots will come to the table arranged in a floral pattern.

Overnight guests are particularly coddled. They have their own dining room upstairs, a charming brown and blue room with a pair of blue-and-white checked sofas in front of a fireplace. Breakfast is brought every morning to the bedroom door. There is a basket with red napkins, a coffee pot, stoneware cups and warm rolls and pastries wrapped in a blue-and-white cloth, all ready to be taken inside for breakfast in bed. On a fine day, if they wish, guests may sit out on the terrace by the little English garden.

Staying at the inn is like spending a weekend in the country with good friends. The Kaufmans leave each room dotted with helpful notes telling the guests where to find things they might need, such as extra blankets.

Over the huge fireplace on the first floor, there is a quotation from the Roman poet Horace: *Ille terrarum mihi praeter omnes angulus ridet*—This corner of earth smiles for me beyond all others.

On his trips between Venusia and Rome, Horace must have stopped off at a country inn that was very much like the Inn at Phillips Mill.

63

CLIFF PARK INN

Milford, Pennsylvania

The Buchanans have been an important family in the Pocono Mountain area of Pennsylvania since the earliest days of the state. George Buchanan, founder of the clan, moved there in 1800 after selling his farm in Newburgh, New York. George was a man of many talents. In addition to owning and operating the Vandermark Hotel in Millford, he was also one of the first judges of the Pike County Court. George combined those two interests nicely. The first sessions of the County Court were held in the hotel's basement, and the cellar of his father-in-law's house was pressed into service as a lockup for debtors. George became known as one of the shrewdest land speculators in the area, often receiving bits of farm acreage in lieu of room rent at the hotel. The Buchanan tradition continued on into this century.

In the early 1900s, however, it appeared the family had made one of its few real-estate mistakes. Harry Winters Buchanan and his wife, Annie Felt Buchanan, had successfully refurbished a capacious old 1820 farmhouse to accommodate guests, but the surrounding farmland was too uneven and rocky to cultivate. It was then that Harry and Annie decided the land might be useful for playing a strange new sport called golf that was just becoming popular in America. Significantly, the nine-hole course, surrounding what is now the Cliff Park Inn, was opened in 1913, the same year American amateur Francis Ouimet won the U.S. Open, beating out two top-ranked British professionals. Golf was suddenly catapulted into the forefront of the American sporting consciousness, and is still a major activity of the inn.

Harry Buchanan, the great-grandson of Harry and Annie, operates the place today with the same easy-going, country club atmosphere of fifty years ago when guests were accommodated by invitation only.

Fore

The unpretentious three-story structure, above, built as a farmhouse in 1820, was transformed into a golfers' haven in the early years of this century. Here, a portion of the rugged, eighty-acre course is framed through a corner of the front terrace.

The Cliff Park Inn is strictly a summer place and is open only during the golfing season from Memorial Day through November.

While not architecturally striking at first glance, the main house is a great, friendly shambles of a building that grows in the affection of all visitors. It is a typical, turn of the century hotel in the Pocono Mountain area. The spacious front veranda runs the full length of the house, recalling summer afternoons when golfers in plus-fours would lounge around on wicker rockers, sipping iced tea and lying about their scores for the day.

Inside are a pair of spectacular sitting rooms. The main salon is large and homey, furnished with seating islands and conversational areas set off by black leather Victorian chaises and hand-painted oil lamps. There is an upright piano in one corner covered with a red, fringed cloth. The room needs only a lovely lady at the keyboard, with her swain turning the pages of a sentimental old Paul Dresser ballad, to complete the nineteenth-century scene.

67

More than meets the eye.

This golf club by day becomes a charming, intimate inn at sundown. Cliff Park has a comfortable, warmly lit main lounge as well as authentic Cordon Bleu cuisine for its guests' enjoyment in the dining room at right, where everyone sits down together at mealtime.

Something for everyone.

Aside from the twelve bedrooms in the main building, the inn offers its guests the privacy of six nearby cottages. The decorations range from the Early American hand-crocheted bedspreads, to an almost neo-Hollywood scalloped floral rug, to the flowered chintzes found in the lounge and bedrooms.

The dining rooms are amiable affairs filled with charming pieces from various periods, but no one is exactly sure which ones. At one end of the room there is a lithograph of an unidentified man with piercing eyes that has been a source of some discussion among the guests for a long time now. The best guess is that he is either Copernicus or Galileo, but the jury is still out on that.

There are twelve generously sized bedrooms upstairs in the main house, and six more in nearby cottages. Tucked around a huge oval of red, yellow and lavender blossoms, the cottages look like the kinds of dressing rooms Gloria Swanson and Pola Negri used to fight over during their heyday as rival silent movie queens on the old Paramount lot. Each one is decorated with the kind of attention to detail that a star appreciates; comfortable furniture, glittering mirrors and copious quantities of fine lace.

Cliff Park Inn has been in the Buchanan family for five generations and is still very much a family operation. Every summer the entire clan reopens the inn for their longtime friends and guests. There is always some kind of friendly bustle going on. The Buchanans seem to be forever doing something extra for their guests. More baths are being added upstairs, so that each bedroom will have its own. Every morning bowls of fresh marigolds appear on the porch. The golf course is being extended to include one water hole that will be an inland version of the famous Pacific ocean-side eighteenth at Pebble Beach.

The Buchanans treat their guests as friends. And, as friends have a way of doing, they keep coming back, season after season. In addition to golf, Cliff Park Inn offers some five hundred acres for hiking. One of the favorite haunts is the cliff from which the inn gets its name. It's a nine hundred-foot drop, and guests can look down on hawks flying above the Delaware River.

69

MAINSTAY INN

Cape May, New Jersey

Located on the southern tip of New Jersey, Cape May is the oldest seaside resort in America. Hundreds of years before the Pilgrims landed at Plymouth Rock, the Absecon Indians regularly left their hunting grounds in the North to take their ease on the cape's hospitable shore. Later, the newly arrived colonials found the place to their liking, and as early as the 1760s, Philadelphia newspaper ads were exhorting their readers to "resort to Cape May."

The cape's real heyday as a resort was in the mid-nineteenth century, when it was the sort of raffish place where newly monied merchants and sporting gentlemen could get in a bit of gambling while their families enjoyed the surf. Mississippi riverboat gamblers would leave the South during the hot summer months and set up shop at one of the three wide-open gambling casinos in Cape May. There was a booming thoroughbred racetrack nearby and, until it burned down in 1878, a pavilion that could accommodate as many as two thousand dancing vacationers.

Some of the social cachet of Cape May has worn off, but its essential charm remains. It is one of the precious few New Jersey resort communities that has been able to survive without turning into another Coney Island. Its chief architectural asset is an area that comprises perhaps the largest single concentration of Victorian homes anywhere in America. The center of town contains every conceivable variation of that spacious building style.

One of the most perfect Victorian structures is the Mainstay Inn, only a few blocks from the ocean. Built in 1872 by some Mississippi gentlemen planters, it was an illicit gaming parlor known as Jackson's Clubhouse. In those days, a sweet, gray-haired old lady would rock all

Live-in museum.

In this largely Victorian town—the inset shows the gingerbread on one of its buildings—the Mainstay is one of the most splendid houses. This elegant mirror, twelve feet high, adorns the front hall.

Jackson's Clubhouse.

For many years, the inn was a gambling club owned by a man named Jackson and was frequented by his cigar-smoking cronies. The inn still has a beautifully furnished game room. In the photo above, the compartmentalized desk was used to hide money as well as hold papers.

day long on its broad veranda, under the overhanging eaves. Her job was to warn the players inside when the police were approaching. The players would then put away the poker cards and pretend to be listening to a musicale. For a while afterwards, the building was a rooming house, and later a local museum.

Today, the place is run by Tom and Sue Carroll, a vibrant young couple in their early thirties, who confess to having worked eighteen hours a day to transform the imposing old structure into a charming inn. Framed by white picket fences and ringed by flower beds, the inn has an impressive pillared cream-colored façade. There is still a good supply of green wicker rocking chairs on the veranda, even though the police come by now just to say hello.

Inside, the Mainstay is a museum one would gladly live in. The rooms are expansively proportioned in the Victorian manner, and a magnificent twelve-foot standing mirror commands the main entrance hall. Each of the main rooms has at least one chandelier. Some are ornate, with copper or wrought-iron images, and others are done in simple, nautical motifs. All are superb examples of Victoriana at its best. There are nine bedrooms upstairs, and impressive affairs they are, furnished with the substantial artifacts that were much admired in the nineteenth century.

Tom and Sue fell in love with Cape May when Tom was stationed there at the local coast guard station, and have become well-informed

Built to last.

In an era when craftsmanship was taken for granted, such articles as the fine brass hardware, above, and the massive bed at right were used as a matter of course in buildings like the Mainstay.

The light of day

pours into the expansively proportioned hall. A ladder in the upstairs hall leads to the light-filled cupola.

Cape May historians. Each bedroom is supplied with a legend about the man to whom it is dedicated. One is named in honor of Henry Clay, who was one of the early champions of Cape May as a resort.

The Mainstay Inn is open to the public in the afternoon for tea, but it does not have a restaurant. Tom and Sue serve only breakfasts to their guests, but the breakfasts are marvelous, homemade country inn fare. Sue does most of the cooking, and Tom helps. One day she might serve strawberry crêpes, and the next, cheese soufflé with fried apples and bacon.

Tom and Sue Carroll are bringing youth and excitement to the traditional art of innkeeping. In the middle of a New Jersey seaside resort, they are creating what they call "a country inn by the sea."

ROBERT MORRIS INN
Oxford, Maryland

The first Robert Morris in Oxford came to the New World in 1738 and arrived in the bustling Maryland seaport to take charge of the American end of a British tobacco importing company. He quickly became the community's leading citizen, taking up residence in the distinguished mansion that still bears his name, and he founded one of the most important families in colonial America.

His son, Robert Morris, was a signer of the Declaration of Independence and a towering figure in the Revolution. Perhaps the richest man in the colonies when the war broke out, he raised millions to help fight the battle for freedom, and when all else failed, he paid General Washington's starving troops out of his own pocket. Morris, however, could apparently manage everybody's money except his own. He eventually went broke as a result of some disastrous land speculations on the western frontier and was sent to debtor's prison. Released in 1801, "without one cent that I can call my own," he lived off the charity of his wife's friends until his death in 1806.

Fortunately, the original Morris family home has been lovingly preserved and maintained as one of the nation's most famous country inns. According to local legend, the house was built by ships' carpenters, and the wood-pegged wall panels bespeak its nautical heritage. The detail work throughout the inn recalls the really remarkable legacy of American craftsmen. The tavern's slate floor was quarried in Vermont, and the Morris family's coat of arms was carved in deep relief from a magnificent, single piece of oak. The four scenes depicted in the dining room—the plains of West Point, an Indian village in Winnipeg, Boston Harbor and the Natural Bridge in Virginia—are all nineteenth-century wallpapers, printed from more than 1,600 woodcuts.

Waterside retreat.

The Robert Morris, above, is located on the Tred Avon River, near the scalloped Chesapeake Bay shore of Maryland. At left, a window in the inn's annex gives a peaceful view of the river through a magnificent stand of old trees on the grounds.

The murals in the dining room are made from nineteenth-century wallpaper samples found in a Philadelphia warehouse several years ago.

Mansard manner.

A bedroom on the Robert Morris's third floor, with a view out onto a watery world.

The winter sun,

overleaf, fades from the sky over the town marina on the Tred Avon River. Some of the area's best sailing occurs in these waters, and twenty-five cents still buys a pleasant ferry ride to Bellevue.

Thanks to innkeepers Ken and Wendy Gibson, the Robert Morris Inn has been converted into a completely modern facility without losing one jot of its original colonial luster. The bedrooms, typical of the style of those days, tend to be a bit quixotic. There are no telephones in any of the rooms, and some of them must share a bath; but each, often with its own fireplace, is a delight in its own way. One room has such a tall, pencil-post bed that guests need special step stairs to get into it. Another features a delightful early trundle bed and an old-fashioned baby basinette. Colorful braided rugs and hanging plants in the windows strike bright and cheerful notes in all the rooms. The inn also runs the Robert Morris Lodge, just down the street. A building with big front porches, it faces the water across grounds that contain a magnificent stand of trees, including a weeping bronze beech.

The restaurant is one of the most famous on the Eastern Shore of Maryland. Oysters à la Gino, an exotic combination of oysters on the half-shell, topped with seasoned crabmeat and broiled with a strip of bacon, is imitated, but never equaled, in kitchens all over the state.

A great variety of people are familiar with the Robert Morris, a somewhat formal country inn in the historic tidewater country. Hunters looking for ducks and geese come in the fall, and yachtsmen come any time of the year that it isn't iced over. Situated directly on the Tred Avon River, the inn has its own anchorage, and many guests miss the traffic on the highways by sailing up from Chesapeake Bay. Once they arrive here, the atmosphere is quiet and the bustle of city life far away.

Southern comfort.

Early in America's national history, this dining room served travelers on the Shenandoah Valley Turnpike. The neat elegance of the room persists into the present. Antique highboys, lowboys, hutches and breakfronts are found throughout the inn, the bounty of a management that prefers the real to a replica. The inn itself, right, has been altered and enlarged through the years and has always stood directly on the roadside, to catch the traveler's eye.

WAYSIDE INN
Middletown, Virginia

Some colonial inns, such as the Griswold in Essex, Connecticut, have stayed almost as they were when they were originally built two centuries ago. The Wayside Inn, however, which first opened its hospitable doors in 1797, has had to change with the times while still striving to maintain its historical traditions.

Located in the lush Shenandoah Valley, the Wayside Inn was first a favorite stopping-off place for rich Virginia planters who came to dine on peanut-fed hams and consume staggering amounts of an incendiary local brand of mint juleps, a drink so popular in the state that English author Frederick Marryat noted,

84

An angelic
companion

hovers over the guests in
the Wayside's bar, a
popular gathering place.

Pride of
the house.

Chef Anna Rose Newman
holds a platter of country
ham, specialty of the
region and of the Wayside.

"You may always know the grave of a Virginian as mint invariably
springs up wherever he is buried."

When the young American nation entered into an era of economic
expansion during the early nineteenth century, the inn became a busy
way station on the Shenandoah Valley Turnpike, offering fresh horses
and a respite for weary stagecoach travelers.

When the Civil War broke out, the inn, then known as Wilkinson's
Tavern, was frequented by soldiers from the North and South alike. It
was at Cedar Creek near Wilkinson's Tavern that one of the most
famous battles of the war was fought. In the last months of the conflict,
the Confederacy's rough old Jubal Early sought to inflict one more loss
on the Union Army. In a cold October dawn, Early's men slipped
through the gorge at Cedar Creek and sent the Yankees reeling in a
surprise attack. What started to be a rout of the Union forces was
stopped when General Phil Sheridan jumped on his black charger,
Rienzi, and dashed towards the battle, leaning low over the saddle,
waving his broadbrimmed hat and shouting, "Turn back! Turn back!"
Sheridan's words and actions steadied his troops and won the day.

That night in the taproom of Wilkinson's Tavern "Sheridan's Ride"
was celebrated joyously; soon, the story of that ride, told and retold,

The fitness of things

at the Wayside includes an English pub sign outside a bedroom with a French armchair, and a canopied bed in a spacious room where the paneled doors are hung on old-fashioned hinges.

became a memorable saga in American folk history. The battle of Cedar Creek has now been re-created in a huge diorama in the Wayside Inn's dining room.

In the twentieth century, Americans took to the road in their automobiles and the Wayside Inn changed its style again, becoming what is generally acknowledged as the first motor inn in the United States.

Given its present name in 1908, the Wayside Inn is now one of the most famous tourist accommodations in the Shenandoah Valley, a comfortable blend of the old and the new where expanded facilities for large groups complement the centuries-old original structure.

The old slave kitchen with its gigantic open-hearth fireplace is now a charming bricked dining room, and the coach yard has been transformed into a cocktail lounge. The rooms in the original building have kept the old, quirky individuality that was common in the days when overnight lodgings were created by craftsmen and not computers.

Today we tend to think of "Early American" as a rigidly maintained style where every piece of furniture in the house came from the same period. In the eighteenth century, of course, there was no such thing as an Early American style. The Virginians of that day gladly mixed their heirlooms from England with their own locally made chairs, tables, cabinets and beds. And those lucky enough to acquire Oriental furniture, bric-a-brac and ornaments that resulted from the China Trade displayed them proudly in their homes. Present-day visitors to the Wayside Inn will find a delightful comingling of American, English and Chinese antiques.

The Wayside Inn sets a good Virginia table, which means that its menu is rich with locally produced meats, poultry and vegetables. Its apple juice, which has been the pride of Virginia for two hundred years, comes right from the Shenandoah Valley, as do its hams, which are all country-cured and processed by neighboring farmers. The distinctive Virginia ham—according to local standards, it must be as spicy as a woman's tongue, as sweet as her kiss and as tender as her love—is one of those happy culinary accidents of the New World. In the middle of the seventeenth century, English piglets let loose on the Virginia countryside began to fatten themselves on local products, especially wild peanuts, which eventually gave the local ham its unique flavor. As with many of the traditional regional dishes served at the Wayside Inn, the hams are prepared according to eighteenth-century recipes: they are soaked overnight and then cooked with dark molasses for extra flavor.

The Wayside Inn maintains its own kitchen garden to ensure historically accurate spicing for special dishes such as chicken gumbo, baked tomatoes, mother-in-law mustard, slave kitchen stew and peanut soup.

All baking is done on the premises and a modern-day guest at the Wayside Inn will understand how the inveterate English traveler George Featherstonhaugh must have felt in 1834, after a tiring coach ride south from Pennsylvania, when he noted in his diary, "I was so exceedingly surprised at seeing on the table a great variety of beautiful-looking bread made both from fine wheaten flour and Indian corn, that I exclaimed, 'Bless me, I must be in Virginia.'"

Pleasures of the season.

A summer playhouse just down the street from the inn is available for guests' entertainment, as is the inn's swimming hole, in an old quarry. There is a gift shop, also. At right is the patio, with the inn's waitresses relaxing over midmorning coffee.

87

88

RED FOX TAVERN

Middleburg, Virginia

Stone showplace.

In the heart of America's most active fox-hunting region, the Red Fox Inn draws regular diners from Washington, forty miles away, as well as local residents, mainly riders. A stone hearth, left, warms the dining room. The building is part of the fabric of colonial Middleburg, so called because it is situated halfway between the port of Alexandria and the inland farming town of Winchester.

The Red Fox Tavern has been part of American social history ever since it served its first tankard of ale in 1728. George Washington surveyed the land and Thomas Jefferson stopped here on his journeys between Monticello and the White House. During the Civil War, the tavern was often used as a Confederate headquarters. Colonel John Mosby and his irregulars planned many of their devastating guerrilla raids here. The bar in the downstairs dining room was made from the field operating table used by the army surgeon serving with Jeb Stuart's cavalry detachment. During the first half of the twentieth century, the spirit was more social than political. The Red Fox was a famous haunt for people interested in horses, and Jacqueline Bouvier Kennedy was a frequent guest. By the mid-1970s, the Red Fox had been through some hard times and had gone to seed. Fortunately, it was bought in 1976 by the energetic Nancy Brown Reuter, a busy Virginia lady with many interests who calls herself the "smallest living conglomerate in the world." Mrs. Reuter and her daughter Diana, a noted interior designer, set to work restoring the Red Fox to its colonial splendor. They went to the restoration at Williamsburg and brought back traditional wallpapers, bedspreads and patterns. They brought antiques from their own home and polished the old place up until it was as bright and shiny as it had been in Jefferson's day. The six upstairs bedrooms are warm and cozy, with braided rugs and patterned wallpapers. Five of the rooms are fitted out with four-poster canopied beds and have their own fireplaces. Mrs. Reuter estimates that she has already spent more than $100,000 on the renovation.

"I just love this part of the countryside, with its old inns and houses," she states. "Somebody was needed to save this inn, and I thought I could do something worthwhile for the community and enjoy myself at the same time. I've tried to make all the work seem like a party."

Thanks to Mrs. Reuter, the Red Fox once again is a busy social center in the heart of the Virginia hunt country. The J. E. B. Stuart Room, with its dark paneling and brace of fireplaces, is the place to meet for a cocktail or a warming cup of tea after an afternoon in the countryside. The Stuart Room is dedicated to good horseflesh, its walls filled with superb oil paintings of hunters and jumpers. This is where the local people gather, and, as one visitor noted, "They come stomping in at all hours, morning and afternoon and evening, talking of horses, nothing but horses, always of horses, forever of horses and horses and horses."

Raising
a standard

to which the weary Virginia traveler may repair, the Red Fox cares mightily about the appointments of its rooms. At left, the J.E.B. Stuart Room—he held a party here—is the perfect place to talk about horses. The guest rooms are simple in design but sumptuous in feeling, with braided rugs and canopied bedsteads.

The main dining room is a classic country restaurant setting with a low, beamed ceiling and freshly painted, white stone walls. "We have cooks, not chefs," says Mrs. Reuter. "We don't try to be a French restaurant." The menu at the Red Fox tends toward solid country food: Brunswick stew, crab cakes, country ham with red-eye gravy and fresh fish. For special parties, the Red Fox will prepare a game dinner of quail, venison, pheasant and duck.

In back of the Red Fox there is a separate cottage known as the Night Fox, where the beat picks up appreciably. It is a combination restaurant and bar much favored by the younger crowd who like their music with charcoal-broiled hamburgers and french fries. The sound is sophisticated, with 67 speakers concealed in two overhead beams. The music may be a bit different now—one of the bartenders is a local disc jockey who plugs in his show directly from the saloon—but the spirit of conviviality is much as it was 250 years ago, when prosperous Virginia planters would stop by to enjoy themselves.

Although there are other activities to pursue in the area, such as tennis and the annual Beagle Trials, sooner or later a visitor to the Red Fox will become involved in horsemanship of one kind or another. The people here still know how to drive a four-in-hand coach, and riding horses can be rented, through the tavern, from the nearby Orchard Hill Stable. Most people come just to watch. There are seven recognized hunts in the surrounding countryside, and horse shows and races are very much a part of the life here.

The Red Fox Tavern is the natural center of Virginia horse country society, and the nearby parking meters are often used as hitching posts. There is a three-foot-high cast-iron jockey out in front of the tavern. Every year it is repainted with the colors of the racing silks of the current winner of the annual Leesburg Gold Cup Race.

Robust refinement.

Food at the Red Fox is plentiful, well prepared, and presented without fuss. Seafood is brought in fresh from Chesapeake Bay. A rich red wine is often served with the roast beef. The dining room furnishings show the graceful strength of colonial Virginia style.

92

94

COUNTRY INN
Berkeley Springs, West Virginia

Berkeley Springs, in West Virginia, is the oldest spa in America. George Washington happened upon its mineral springs in 1748 and enjoyed their healing properties so much he built a summer home here after his return from the Revolution in 1784. The springs were a great favorite of many important patriots in the early days of the republic. True to the egalitarian spirit of the times, the first state park in the nation's history was established here when a fifty-acre section with its own spring was set aside for "poor and infirm people and suffering humanity." People have been coming here for help or simple relaxation ever since.

One of the landmarks of Berkeley Springs is the Country Inn, built in 1933, just a few yards from the original spring. The present owners, Jack and Adele Barker, first came to the Country Inn as guests in the early 1970s. Adele was recuperating from an accident; Jack was a retired schoolmaster. They spent an entire summer at the inn, and when it was up for sale in 1972, Jack decided to step out of retirement and "start perking again."

The inn is a solid, three-story house with six white pillars in front that give a somewhat formal look to the establishment. Actually, it is a charmingly furnished country home built for comfort and filled with family touches the Barkers brought with them. Jim is a deft maker of collages; several examples of his handiwork, combining musical instruments with old musical scores, are around the house. The dining room is a high-ceilinged room with white walls dramatically highlighted by dark wood paneling. Running around the entire circumference of the room is a single shelf of antiques and assorted knickknacks, including clocks, coffee tins, pitchers, baskets and tea kettles. The inn specializes in down-home country cooking and serves three hefty meals

95

Innocent aboard.

Kevin, son of manager William North, is on hand to greet guests at the Country Inn. Berkeley Springs is also known as Bath, for its natural mineral springs. The mayor of the original Bath, England, sends the inn a small commemorative gift each year.

The Berkeley Room, *overleaf,* provides the setting for an exciting game of bridge.

a day. The Berkeley Room downstairs is a large open area used for card games and general recreation. The Barkers keep a large supply of board games on hand, including puzzles, Chinese checkers, Scrabble, Monopoly and checkers.

Although all the standard resort-type attractions are in the area, such as golf, tennis, hunting and fishing, the springs are the principal attraction. The health spa is operated by the state. In addition to enjoying the famous spring waters, guests can get a massage and mineral bath for less than ten dollars a day.

As close as they are to the springs, Jack and Adele have a hard time finding the time to get over there. There is always something to do around the place, and Jack spends much of his day in overalls working with his chief handyman, seeing to the endless rounds of maintenance required. The two of them have completed a private chalet for the Barkers just a few steps above the inn.

"Jack dreams and dreams," says Adele pragmatically, "and some of it even gets done."

Relax and go shopping.

The Morgan Room, barely visible at left of photo through the glass panes of the comfortable living room, is a small country store.

Accidental collage.

The inn's bulletin board, at right, gives a clue as to how owner Jack Barker passes his spare time. Mr. Barker's collages have been featured locally and decorate the inn.

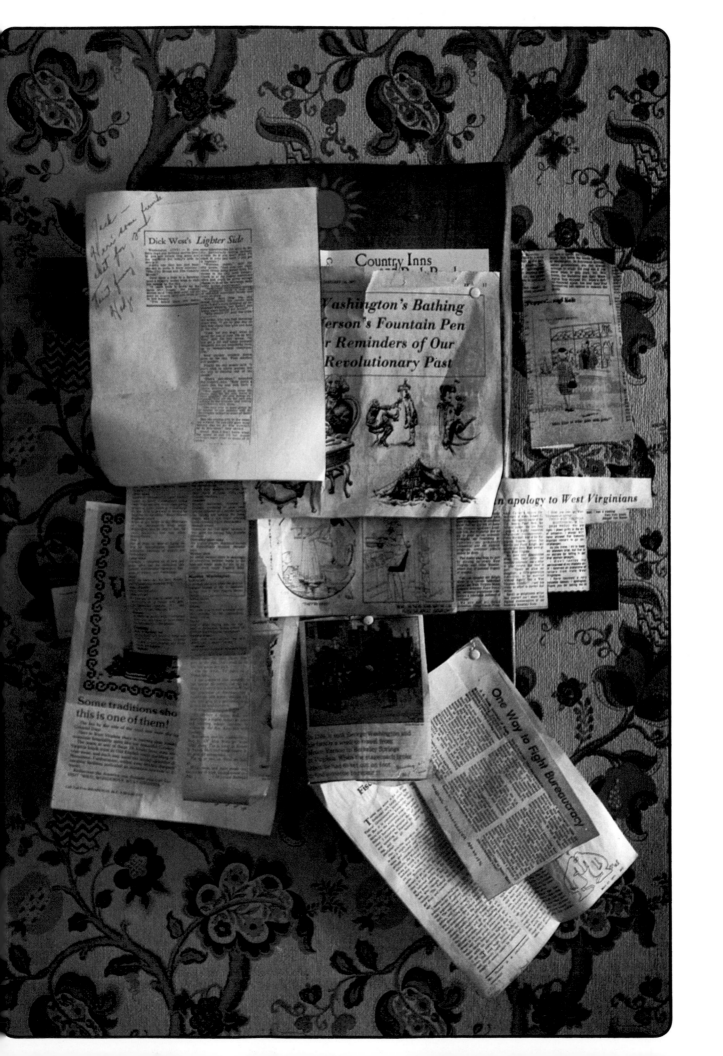

NU-WRAY INN

Burnsville, North Carolina

In a sentimental mood.

Seen from the town square at night, the three-storied inn, above, appears a stately old establishment. This antique cuckoo clock, a favorite among the inn's collection, is from the Black Forest.

Burnsville was first settled by Daniel Boone and his people, but it was named after War of 1812 veteran Otway Burns. He was active in Carolina politics and cast the deciding vote in the state legislature that created Yancey County. Local citizens not only named their town after him, they put up a statue in his honor on the village square.

The square is a vintage piece of nineteenth-century Americana. At one end of the green is the Yancey County Country Store, run by Captain George Downing, who presides over an almost incalculable amount of clutter. Bolts of calico, dulcimers, handmade soaps, sassafras jelly, freshly ground peanut butter, corncob back-scratchers, Armenian cracker bread, corn-husk dolls, sealing wax and 185 different items that start with the letter *B* are just part of the inventory that is stuffed into some fourteen rooms at Captain Downing's emporium.

Commanding the square from the other end is the Nu-Wray Inn, a landmark in Burnsville since 1867, when Garrett T. Ray first expanded an old eight-room log cabin and turned it into Ray's Inn. Mr. Ray's daughter Julia married William Wray, and in 1917 they took over after renaming the inn. Change, however, comes slowly in the Smoky Mountains, and there are still a few old-timers in the area who refer to the Nu-Wray Inn as "the new Wray place in the old Ray place."

By whatever name, it is a big, comfortable three-story country house that has been providing down-home hospitality for more than one hundred years. When innkeeper Rush Wray and his sister Annie Wray Bennett summon guests for dinner, it is time for some fancy country eating. As many as twenty dishes are served on the three long tables in the dining room, where everybody eats family-style. The house

The Shadow knew

this magnificent Stromberg-Carlson radio, as did Jack Benny, Charlie McCarthy and hosts of families in the 1930s, when radio was a prime source of evening entertainment. More modern diversions are available in the inn's living room, above, but the setting is still one of gracious southern conviviality.

specialty is smoked, cured ham dipped in a sauce of molasses, brown sugar and red pepper. There are piles of chicken with cornbread stuffing and milk gravy; sweet and sour beef stew; baked beans; candied yams; and bowls of such locally grown vegetables as summer squash, turnip greens, tomatoes, corn on the cob and snap beans. Annie Wray Bennett makes stacks of biscuits served with fresh, country butter. People have been raving about them for years, and she doesn't understand why. "They're just plain old homemade biscuits," she protests. After dinner has been topped off with dishes of homemade ice cream, there is a very slow, tottering exodus to the high-backed rocking chairs out on the front porch.

The Nu-Wray is a house that loves music. Instead of using the traditional dinner bell to announce supper, Rush plays a tune on a German-built Reginaphone music box. During the meal, he sets the Steinway Duo-Art player piano in the music room to work playing piano rolls of every form of music, from jazz and honky-tonk to Liszt and Chopin.

The furnishings at the Nu-Wray are good, solid country pieces, with the emphasis on comfort rather than on great style. The downstairs sitting room is very relaxing, with an oversized stone fireplace at one

104

end and a particularly fine deacon's chair with patchwork pillows. Daniel Boone VII, a direct descendant, made the ironwork for the fireplace and the overhead lighting fixtures, as well. The room also houses charming collections of corn-husk dolls, quilts and pillows made by the local women. The upstairs parlor, called the Blue Room, is a treasure house of old-fashioned country furnishings: an 1834 Gale & Company piano that still plays if one is *very* gentle; a standing Tiffany lamp in its original, unelectrified condition; a spinning wheel; and a sofa that was converted from a cooling board (used at the turn of the century to lay out the body of the deceased).

Inside originals.

The furnishings are old-fashioned and unassuming. The hutch, left, houses some of the inn's crystal, while the Blue Room, a parlor, contains this Victorian chair.

Big man in town.

The town square of Burnsville, at left, features this statue of the town's namesake, General Otway Burns. The Nu-Wray stands across the square from the Yancey County Country Store, where the proprietor's wife is shown behind the counter.

The Nu-Wray also contains a delightful collection of cuckoo clocks amassed by the Wray family over the years. There is one particularly magnificent specimen in the downstairs parlor with bird and rabbit carvings from the Black Forest. Together, they set up a happy clatter that moved one guest to compose:

> *This little inn has many cuckoo clocks*
> *That all night long their plaintive notes repeat.*
> . . . . .
> *Back in the city with its ceaseless roar,*
> *Dreaming, I hear the cuckoo clocks call once more.*

Gentle breeding lingers into age . . .

at the Swordgate. Built in the early 1800s, it was named for the Sword Gate, at left, the regal entrance to Sword Gate House. The inn and the house were originally part of the same complex. In the heart of Charleston's historic district, the inn is now a recognized landmark.

Southern belle.

Overleaf. The elegant ballroom was once the scene of sumptuous parties during the inn's early days as a private residence. Wide doorways and large open spaces accommodated the ladies' hoop skirts.

SWORDGATE INN

Charleston, South Carolina

The Swordgate Inn, a tiny little bandbox of a place situated in the heart of Charleston's historic district, is a nineteenth-century guest house with a score of charming grace notes.

Upon entering the inn after a long journey, guests know immediately that they have a conscientious host. A cut-glass decanter of Sherry and two glasses wait in each guest room, together with a bowl of fruit and a vase of fresh flowers. The four bedrooms on the ground floor have the graciousness of a century-old establishment, offset by vibrant modern

**Sunshine
and scones**
are served outside for
breakfast when the
weather is clear. Guests
help themselves to a
sideboard laden with
traditional southern
breakfast fare.

color coordination and accessories. The rooms are filled with attractive linens, ruffled pillows, coverlets in bright fabrics and upholstered chairs. The baths have thick towels in lime and mint green. The top-floor bedroom is the most elegant. Its high ceiling accommodates a lofty, four-poster bed with a hand-crocheted canopy of incredible intricacy made entirely of tobacco tying threads. There is also a lovely, formal fireplace with a sterling silver poker.

The Swordgate Inn serves a hearty Charleston breakfast, one of the finest in the South. Innkeeper Kerry Anderson gets up at 6:30 to prepare the morning's feast. The dining area is tiny, just four tables with green-and-white checked tablecloths in a narrow room that sometimes doubles as Kerry's office. When the weather is accommodating, as it often is, everyone goes out on the patio, with its wrought-iron tables and garden chairs, and eats under the morning sun. But wherever it is served, breakfast at the Swordgate Inn is always a treat. Guests serve themselves from a sideboard laden with a variety of southern breakfast specialties, including baked apples, scrambled eggs, cheese omelets, baked ham, pastries and cheeses, fresh orange juice and plenty of fragrant coffee and homemade biscuits. Kerry simmers the grits all night and serves them with butter and cinnamon, the latter in a silver shaker.

Although the inn is quite small, there are two opulent rooms on the second floor—a formal dining room, and a magnificent ballroom that is a regular stop on the annual Charleston House Tours. In 1977, the Preservation Society of Charleston held a candlelit ceremony in the gilded ballroom, where five musicians performed on recorders for some five hundred visitors. In the daytime, the sun streams through the twelve-foot windows, and a gigantic, gilt-edged French mirror reflects almost the whole room. Kerry uses the room occasionally for parties and receptions.

The house was built in the early 1800s as a residence and was once the home of the British consul. Later on, it was part of Madame Talvande's School for Young Ladies.

Few cities in America have protected their historic areas more carefully than Charleston. More than fifty pre-Revolutionary buildings in mint condition exist in the city, but Charleston's particular pride is the nineteenth-century English townhouse architecture that gives the city its distinctive ambiance.

The Swordgate Inn has a rack of bicycles for the use of its guests, but it is just as easy to walk around the area. There are forty-nine historic sights listed in the *Chamber of Commerce Visitor's Guide* to the old city; thirty of them are within five blocks of the inn.

Stars at Heaven's border.

This hand-crocheted string canopy, with its intricate star pattern, was made from tobacco tying cord by a woman in payment of her husband's dental bill.

Splendor in isolation.

Live-oak trees, above, form a natural canopy over the roads of Cumberland Island, off the Georgia coast. Greyfield, the former home of the Thomas Carnegie family, preserves a tradition of American leisure in this setting of natural beauty. The living room, at left, contains objects collected by the family.

Overleaf: woody vines thread the live oaks near the entrance to Greyfield.

GREYFIELD INN

Cumberland Island, Georgia

The Greyfield Inn is like no other place in America. Half the time, it can't be reached by telephone, and when people write ahead for reservations, as often as not they receive instead a request for references. When they are finally accepted as guests, they will find that the Greyfield Inn is almost impossible to get to—a boat and a chartered airplane are the only means. Once they arrive at Greyfield, if the guests are looking for traditional resort activities, they will find there is practically nothing to do. There are no golf courses nearby, no tennis courts on the property and no swimming pool. Yet despite all this, or perhaps because of it, Greyfield is one of the most memorable country inns on the eastern seaboard. What guests do find when they come to Greyfield is a gracious, richly appointed private home, fine food and one of the few patches of completely unspoiled wilderness left in America.

Greyfield was built around the turn of the century as the island hideaway of Thomas Carnegie, Andrew's brother. It was the Carnegie

home for generations and is still owned by Lucy Ferguson, Thomas's granddaughter. Mrs. Ferguson, who could live anywhere in the world, so loves Cumberland Island she remains here year-round in her own home just a short walk from Greyfield, one of the dozen or so permanent residents on the island. Greyfield became an inn in the 1960s when Mrs. Ferguson decided to allow a few of her friends to come to the island as paying guests. Although people outside the immediate Carnegie social circle are now also sometimes among the seventeen guests Greyfield can accommodate at any one time, it is still very much a family-type affair.

Guests are ushered into a fine old home. The living room is paneled in dark wood offset with bright, rustic colors. While a fire crackles on the oversized hearth, guests are free to have a cup of tea in one of the Morris chairs or just lounge around on the sofa, reading a book from the Carnegies' library just down the hall. Greyfield is filled with family memorabilia: stacks of old photograph albums of the Carnegies at play in the early part of the twentieth century; hundreds of varieties of seashells gathered during family excursions over the island; and a shelf full of sports trophies from long-forgotten country club tournaments.

A major event at Greyfield is dinner, served buffet-style from a huge

Richness in reserve.

Greyfield is as much a chronicle of an important American family as it is an inn. Memorabilia on display include a photo on a table in the living room of a clan gathering, above. The library at right contains a number of signed first editions.

The past in place.

The house is unaltered and is maintained much as it was when the Carnegies lived there. The bedroom shown in two views here was used for many years by Lucy Ferguson, Thomas Carnegie's granddaughter and the present owner of Greyfield. She is pictured with her two sisters in a portrait over the bed. The bedroom is part of a suite that includes its own sitting room.

mahogany sideboard in the main dining room. There is no permanent chef; so the food varies from week to week, as various local cooks come over from the mainland to prepare their specialties—rack of lamb, one of the many local game birds or any of a variety of regional fish. The special treat of the house is roast suckling pig.

The upstairs rooms vary greatly, from relatively small to one baronial sleeping chamber fitted out with a massive bed that is covered with the same white spread Mrs. Ferguson had as a child.

If there is little in the way of organized recreational activity at Greyfield Inn, Cumberland Island itself is a nature lover's paradise. The few inland roads cut like tunnels through the stands of live oak, whose sprawling limbs cast a soft, teal-blue shadow over the island. On the strand, the ever-shifting sand dunes on this totally undeveloped island give the sense of a place that is immutable yet constantly changing. More than three hundred different species of birds have been identified on Cumberland Island. Inland, wild ponies and pigs share the island with deer, armadillos, alligators and wild turkeys. Hiking, shelling, beachcombing and birdwatching are the staple activities at Greyfield. As they say on Cumberland Island, "The only recreational director here is Mother Nature." She certainly puts on a wonderful show for Greyfield's guests.

CHALET SUZANNE

Lake Wales, Florida

Florida fantasy.

Chalet Suzanne, on the shores of a Florida lake, is an exciting mélange of outré architecture, edgy color and startling objects. The painted skillet at left has sentimental value for innkeeper Vita Hinshaw, a former stewardess, who used it to scramble eggs for her passengers. The artist, Paul Norman, worked for the airline catering company and painted it for her. A famous house specialty, inset, is the cinnamon-broiled grapefruit with sautéed chicken livers.

Long before Walt Disney World came to Florida, there was the Chalet Suzanne. A funky jumble of turrets, minarets, towers and heaven knows what else, Chalet Suzanne is the sort of place where one would expect Dorothy to stop for lunch on her way to find the Wizard of Oz. It is a wonderfully wacky confusion of architectural and decorative styles, where nothing makes sense but everything works. The Swiss Dining Room is decorated in a profusion of Oriental tiles, and the Round Room is heptagonal. Huge, deep ashtrays are used as soup bowls, and doubtlessly there are some soup bowls that are being used as ashtrays. One restaurant critic noted, "The only thing you can rely on is that the flatware will never match anything else on the table, not even the other forks and spoons."

The chalet also boasts one of the most theatrical flourishes to be found in any dining room in America—its Honeymoon Suite. Built one level up in the dining room, it contains a table for two on a curtained balcony, where a couple can overlook the rest of the room yet maintain absolute privacy. They don't even have to be disturbed by waiters bringing their order; they can hoist it up themselves in a glass-enclosed dumbwaiter.

As enchanting as it is, the Chalet Suzanne is much more than just an unusually strange inn with idiosyncratic furnishings. It is also a fine overnight accommodation, and a first-class restaurant with an international reputation for culinary excellence. *New York Times* critic Craig Claiborne placed Chalet Suzanne in the first rank of restaurants around the world.

This gentle dreamland of a place, which looks as if it were created with a wave of Billie Burke's magic wand, is actually the result of more

than forty years of hard work by a very tough-minded lady. In 1931, when America was in the grip of the Great Depression, Bertha Hinshaw was a widow with two children to look after, and no job. To support her family, she turned her home into a tiny restaurant and did all the cooking herself in a twelve-foot kitchen. Bertha had a natural eye for the business. Customers were willing to come long distances for Bertha's superb cooking, so the chatelaine added overnight guest facilities to allow them to stay even longer. Today, Chalet Suzanne has thirty guest rooms, and the restaurant seats 150 dinner guests.

As the chalet, named after her daughter, prospered, Bertha scoured the world looking for antiques, artifacts and art objects for it. She was especially fond of tiles and brought home profusions of them in every style. She once spent days in North Africa watching workmen razing

Heady combinations.

Excellent food in startling surroundings is a Chalet Suzanne hallmark. The Round Dining Room overlooks Lake Suzanne. If consistency of style is disregarded in the furnishings, consistent high quality in the food is not.

Some of the chalet's famous dishes are seen at right: Chicken Suzanne, top, served—like all the meals at Chalet Suzanne— with mint sherbet to clear the palate; Romaine soup, served in Norwegian ashtrays, center; and curried shrimp with orange rice, served with a tray of condiments, bottom.

Got a match?

The Swiss Dining Room, at left, is decorated with Oriental tiles. At Chalet Suzanne nothing matches, yet everything fits. Often the silverware at one table is of several different patterns, and the china varies as well. Each piece is fascinating when not simply beautiful.

a mosque. As the men knocked down the precious tiles, Bertha ran around below stuffing them into an umbrella and made off with them. Some of the most magnificently tiled bath facilities one is likely to see this side of Mecca are testimony to Bertha's energies as a tile collector. Clearly, she had broad tastes and collected many different styles. Glassware, furniture and chandeliers from every corner of the globe make their happy home at Chalet Suzanne.

In a single room there are no less than eight different kinds of lighting fixtures: a richly colored Tiffany lamp; a heavy, wrought-iron Spanish lantern; a Venetian glass grape lamp; a French globe; a hexagonal English lantern; a jeweled lamp from Baghdad; a ship's lantern from Singapore; and a Spanish night guard's pole lamp from Toledo. Each table is set with a different china pattern: Spode, Royal Doulton, Wedgwood and Royal Windsor, as well as numerous other patterns from Italy, Portugal, Norway, Sweden, Japan and the Netherlands. Stemware varies from graceful Italian wine glasses to elegant nine-inch blue goblets to tiny, hand-painted, tulip-shaped glasses. One of the most striking conversation pieces in the chalet is a beautiful, luminous, stained-glass window of a shamrock inside a Star of David. There is a perfectly good explanation for this unusual combination, but no one at Chalet Suzanne has the foggiest idea what it might be.

The chalet has built its formidable reputation on food. In contrast to the somewhat giddy surroundings, the menu seems to be rather straightforward, offering traditional-sounding dishes. But nothing is traditional at Chalet Suzanne, and every dish comes from a special family recipe. One unusual specialty is an intriguing creation in which a grapefruit half is broiled with sugar, melted butter and cinnamon and then topped off with a portion of sautéed chicken livers. Chicken Suzanne is another specialty of the house—the chicken is baked and

The photographs show exterior and interior views of the Governor Suite. Matters of state might seem less pressing here than back at the office.

repeatedly basted in its own natural juices until it is glazed to a deep, dark amber, and the meat comes away from the bone at the touch of a fork. Served by pretty waitresses in colorful Scandinavian costumes, meals at Chalet Suzanne are feasts at which the guests are scandalously indulged. Mint sherbet is served with the main course for clearing the palate, and a rich crêpe Suzanne, with an orange and lemon sauce, is served just before the actual dessert.

From the start, the chalet was famous for its soups. So much so, they opened a cannery and went into business with their own Chalet Suzanne

129

Trial by tile.

Bertha Hinshaw, who collected the elements that went into Chalet Suzanne, and then directed their installation, was reputedly very difficult to work for. The splendid tub, above, and the wash basin, below, made from a china bowl, are each obviously one of a kind.

Altered perceptions

of the world are the likely result of a few days spent in the Governor Suite, above right, or the Orchid Room, below.

brand of soups that is now sold worldwide in gourmet shops. **Astronaut** James Irwin was so fond of the Romaine soup—a subtle blending **of** chicken broth, chopped spinach, mushrooms, carrots, onions **and** herbs—that he took some with him aboard Apollo 16 and drank it **on** the moon.

Chalet Suzanne is now operated by Bertha's son Carl, his wife, Vita, and their children Tina and Eric. Long active in the management of the chalet, Carl brings just the right kind of Renaissance talents needed to run such an eclectic establishment. An administrator, he runs the cannery, supervising the production of the house-brand soups and other gourmet specialties. An artist, he painted all the murals in the bar, Austrian winter scenes, in an easy, freehand style. A former P-51 fighter pilot, he has made the chalet a particular favorite with pilots. About twenty-five percent of their business, Carl estimates, flies in directly and lands on the chalet's private landing strip. A master cook, Carl is often in the kitchen, working in a flight suit, making sure the sauces are just right.

Carl and Vita were childhood sweethearts. They met on a school bus that was taking them to class in the fifth grade. Together, they carry on the tradition of fine service and gracious accommodation started by Bertha. The Chalet Suzanne requires a tremendous amount of personal attention, but Carl and Vita are thinking about expanding with another restaurant, possibly in Fort Lauderdale.

132

"Some of our friends are retiring," Carl points out, "but we feel like we're just starting."

Plane and fancy.

Chalet Suzanne has its own private airstrip, right. The elaboration of the complex is obviously the result of a special vision of what pleasure can be. A broad patio, below, stretches between buildings housing the inn's guest rooms.

ROD AND GUN LODGE

Everglades City, Florida

The Florida Everglades seem quite apart from the rest of the United States. One of the few subtropical regions in our country, this 5,000-square-mile expanse of junglelike swamp looks more like part of a South Pacific island than a tourist attraction in the Sunshine State. The Everglades is a place of awesome beauty. Orchids grow wild among the lacy cypress trees, and towering mangroves reach seventy feet into the sky. Alligators, otters, manatees and giant turtles live in its murky waters; broad-winged snake birds fly overhead. It can also be a dark and mysterious hiding place. At the start of the Seminole Wars in 1835, thousands of Indians drifted into the Everglades and lived there for generations, defying the best efforts of the United States Army to root them out. During the Civil War, it provided a haven for Union sympathizers within the secessionist state who learned to live in the wild until the end of hostilities.

For nature lovers and sportsmen today, the Everglades is a bountiful paradise, offering sights unseen anywhere else in America and some of the best fishing in the world. The premier inn in this exotic country is the Rod and Gun Lodge, located less than a mile from the entrance to the Everglades National Park. A rambling, two-story house of white cypress, the lodge has been an exclusive sportsmen's hideaway for the last eighty years. It is a particular favorite with high-level government officials, who come south to get away from Washington and try the fishing in the warm Florida waters. Presidents Truman, Eisenhower and Nixon were great fans of the lodge, and Chief Justice Warren Burger is a frequent guest. Although most guests drive to the Rod and Gun Lodge from Miami or Fort Lauderdale, some fly their own planes to the nearby, twenty-five hundred-foot municipal landing strip.

A formal approach

to living the sporting life is customary at the Rod and Gun Lodge. The curved stairs at left lead to the dining room. The lodge's dramatic glassed-in swimming pool, above, sets off the lush tropical environment. Facing Florida's Ten Thousand Islands on the Gulf of Mexico, the inn's marina, *overleaf,* is a popular anchorage for boats traveling the irregular coastline of southwest Florida.

Bogie
was
here,

or seems not far away,
amid the cypress walls,
fishing trophies and wood-
bladed overhead fans of
this tropical hideaway.

Guests approaching the Rod and Gun Lodge today get the feeling of coming upon a country club that really is in the country. In front, there is a huge banyan tree, with a trunk fifteen feet around, and a clump of bamboo rustling in the breeze. White-pileated woodpeckers dart brightly about. The clubhouse has a cheerful yellow and white awning over-hanging the curved brick stairway that leads to a front porch filled with rocking chairs. Inside, it looks like a warm and comfortable hunting lodge, which it was until the Park Service outlawed all hunting in the Everglades twenty-five years ago. There is a cozy, cypress-paneled bar, decorated with stuffed fish, where anglers can gather for a cocktail in the evening and tell one another stories of what would have been the biggest catch of the season if it hadn't gotten away. Beyond the large hearth in the center of the lobby is a massive pool table with a stuffed alligator eight feet long suspended from the ceiling.

The dining room is the most formal part of the Rod and Gun Lodge. The walls are made of soft, pecky cypress, once considered a cheap local lumber, but now a highly prized wood. The room is furnished with comfortable club chairs, and chandeliers glow softly overhead. The restaurant is one of the most famous in southern Florida. Its menu consists of straightforward but beautifully prepared dishes with the emphasis on seafood. The stone crab and the sea scallops are house specialties, and there is always a delicious fish of the day from local waters, often a succulent grouper. For five dollars, the Rod and Gun Lodge will cook to order anything guests catch. It's a great treat when a guest brings back a freshly caught snook. Although it is not permitted

Warm sun.

The reflective white of a sunstruck exterior porch is cut only partially by an overhead canopy.

for a restaurant in Florida to have snook on the menu, it is perfectly legal for the establishment to cook it for anyone who has caught one.

Even the most incompetent angler should be able to bring some fresh fish home for dinner. The Rod and Gun Lodge is only a few yards away from its own marina on the Barron River and is directly across from part of the Ten Thousand Islands, a curved and crazy coastline that literally teems with fish. There are some fifty varieties within fifteen miles of the lodge, including grouper, bank fish, redfish, trout, snook and the sporting tarpon.

There are other recreational facilities for the guests, as well. One can enjoy the sunny, screened-in swimming pool or use the pair of nearby town tennis courts.

But innkeeper Martin Bowen says that most of his guests are there just to fish. And why not? One guest caught several red snapper without even leaving the marina. As he said, "You just throw your line out and pull them in. It's as simple as that."

Warm welcome.

Inside the paneled darkness of the lobby, all is luxe and calm. The old-fashioned telephone booth is conspicuously placed, but what taking a call here lacks in privacy is made up in charm.

LAMOTHE HOUSE
New Orleans, Louisiana

On Esplanade, at the edge of the French Quarter, the Lamothe's double townhouse is a gem of New Orleans architecture. In the upstairs hall is a richly upholstered French sofa, above. The inset shows the figured globe of an old kerosene lamp.

The Florida Everglades seem quite apart from the rest of the United States. One of the few subtropical regions in our country, this 5,000-square-mile expanse of junglelike swamp looks more like part of a South Pacific island than a tourist attraction in the Sunshine State. The Everglades is a place of awesome beauty. Orchids grow wild among the lacy cypress trees, and towering mangroves reach seventy feet into the sky. Alligators, otters, manatees and giant turtles live in its murky waters; broadwinged snake birds fly overhead. It can also be a dark and mysterious hiding place. At the start of the Seminole Wars in 1835, thousands of Indians drifted into the Everglades and lived there for generations, defying the best efforts of the United States Army to root them out. During the Civil War, it provided a haven for Union sympathizers within the secessionist state who learned to live in the wild until the end of hostilities.

For nature lovers and sportsmen today, the Everglades is a bountiful paradise, offering sights unseen anywhere else in America and some of the best fishing in the world. The premier inn in this exotic country is the Rod and Gun Lodge, located less than a mile from the entrance to the Everglades National Park. A rambling, two-story house of white cypress, the lodge has been an exclusive sportsmen's hideaway for the last eighty years. It is a particular favorite with high-level government officials, who come south to get away from Washington and try the fishing in the warm Florida waters. Presidents Truman, Eisenhower and Nixon were great fans of the lodge, and Chief Justice Warren Burger is a frequent guest. Although most guests drive to the Rod and Gun Lodge from Miami or Fort Lauderdale, some fly their own planes to the nearby, 2,500-foot municipal landing strip.

An age of grace

is evident in the dining room, setting for the inn's *petit déjeuner*. The bedroom at right opens out onto the central courtyard.

Each room is suffused with traditional southern charm but has been complemented with the modern conveniences: private baths, air conditioning and room telephones. Although Lamothe House could operate year-round, it is closed in July and August for refurbishing.

The animating spirit of Lamothe House is eighty-four-year-old Gertrude Munson, who has been here for almost twenty-five years. She has recently given over the day-to-day innkeeping operation to her daughter-in-law Mrs. Kenneth Langguth, but Mrs. Munson is still very active around the hotel. An authentic New Orleans belle in her day, she was mistress of Glenwood Plantation on Bayou La Fourche for many years before returning to her native city. She comes to breakfast, the only meal served at Lamothe House, whenever she can, and turns *petit déjeuner* into a proper New Orleans salon. After the guests are introduced to one another, conversation moves along brightly. Breakfast is supposed to be served from nine to ten, but frequently it lasts much longer. Guests are loath to leave the long banquet table, where hot coffee laced with chicory is poured from a two-hundred-year-old Sheffield urn.

The big sleep.

Named for a renowned New Orleans cabinetmaker, the Mallard Room features several of his pieces, including this magnificent bed with its high canopy.

The French Quarter, one of the most magnetic attractions of the South, is only a few blocks away. Guests may stroll through the French Market, browse among the shops on Royal Street, take in the thumping Dixieland jazz joints on Bourbon Street or visit the awesome St. Louis Cathedral.

But nowhere is the spirit of old New Orleans more perfectly captured than at Lamothe House on one of those special occasions when Mrs. Munson can be talked into preparing her special recipe for *Café Brûlot*. Mrs. Munson has become a legend in New Orleans for this exotic concoction of flaming brandy and coffee, laced with spices, cinnamon, cloves, lemon peel and sugar, which she serves in the grand manner. All the lights are turned out, and the room is illuminated by a dancing blue flame as Mrs. Munson prepares her glorious brew. It is the delightful light of traditionally elegant New Orleans hospitality.

MAISON DE VILLE

New Orleans, Louisiana

Heart of the matter.

The courtyard at the Maison de Ville, with its cast-iron fountain, fish pond and semitropical plants, is the centerpiece of a small hotel where luxury and individualized service are part of the charm. In the morning, fresh croissants and New Orleans coffee, accompanied by a fresh rose, are served to guests in their rooms. They may also breakfast on the patio or in the parlor.

Old World elegance and attentive Continental service make up the prevailing spirit at the Maison de Ville. Overnight guests are pampered from the moment the houseman takes their luggage and car keys until he returns the car at the end of their stay. Walking in the narrow entryway past an arched window, guests are welcomed by an attractive desk clerk, who, before they can even check in, will ask if she can take care of their dinner reservations at any one of the famous New Orleans restaurants within a few blocks of the Maison de Ville.

149

The hotel's interior boasts some of the most historic architecture in the Vieux Carré. The original slave quarters date back to the 1740s and are thought to be among the oldest buildings in New Orleans. Built as a private home, the Maison de Ville has had a long and exciting social history. One of the owners in the nineteenth-century was Mr. A. Peychaud, a noted pharmacist of the time, who, according to New Orleans legend, was home one evening fooling around with a collection of his medicinal bitters. He added a dash of this and a pinch of that to a measure of bourbon, and the next thing he knew, he had invented the potent Sazerac, one of the world's first known cocktails.

The Maison de Ville still exudes the ambiance of an elegant New Orleans townhouse. The courtyard is a classic French Quarter resting place, where guests can sit under the cooling trees. In the center, there is a triple-tiered cast-iron fountain that sends cascades of water into a goldfish pond. The rooms in the main house are among the finest in the city. The downstairs salon is furnished with exquisite French-accented pieces, set formally in a room of muted gold and brown, highlighted by antique mirrors and marble fireplaces. The bedrooms are meticulously furnished with eighteenth- and nineteenth-century antiques,

French accent.

The salon at Maison de Ville, left and above, is appointed with French furniture of the eighteenth and nineteenth centuries. A somewhat shabby rooming house before its restoration ten years ago, the hotel now displays some of the most carefully finished interiors in the city. Refreshments—coffee, tea, Sherry, Port, soft drinks, fruit—are *lagniappe* (complimentary), a New Orleans tradition.

towering four-posters, marble basins and antique brass fittings.

Separate from the main house, in the rear of the courtyard, are what once were the slave quarters. These somewhat raffish rooms have been great favorites of writers. Tennessee Williams completed the final draft of his great play *A Streetcar Named Desire* while staying in Room 9.

A block and a half away is a small cluster of houses, operated by the Maison de Ville, that offers an incredibly luxurious, urban living experience. Six cottages, some of them dating back to the days of the first Spanish settlers, are clustered behind a hundred-year-old stucco wall. The cottage area is named for John James Audubon, who came to New Orleans in 1821 and took up residence with his family in the little house on rue Dauphine. Renowned as the most popular wildlife artist of his time, Audubon created many of his best-loved drawings here. His house sets the tone for the rest of the complex. Of half-timbered brick construction, it is a charmingly informal Creole version of the half-timbered houses of Europe. Today, the original cottages, joined by contemporary but complementary structures, have been completely renovated into modern living accommodations. Each of the cottages has at least one bedroom and a kitchen—which the hotel keeps

New Orleans primitive.

The French Quarter is a mélange of many cultural elements, yet keeps its own character to this day. The ancient *briquette entre poteaux* construction of the inn's Audubon cottages, left, makes a splendid backdrop for their rich furnishings. A room in the hotel itself, right, has a balcony overlooking rue Toulouse.

The basket of fruit on the inn's etched-glass front door, above, offers a symbolic welcome.

stocked with soft drinks, lemons and mixers—and its own private courtyard and flower garden. The cottages all share a modern, crystal-clear swimming pool in an area of old brick set off by graceful statuary.

No matter where guests stay, they will be constantly cared for with unobtrusive European-style service. The Maison de Ville employs a ubiquitous concierge to book dinner reservations, advise on shopping and arrange sightseeing tours. In fact, the concierge will do everything just like his Parisian counterpart except gossip with the neighbors and steam open the mail. The hotel has also preserved that all-but-forgotten custom of shining shoes that have been left outside the bedroom doors. The complimentary Continental breakfast is served with a flourish.

154

The courtyard,

has many moods. The old slave quarters off the courtyard, right, also contain rooms. Tennessee Williams is thought to have worked on *A Streetcar Named Desire* in one of them.

Every morning each guest is presented with a silver tray bearing freshly squeezed orange juice, flaky croissants, a pot of fragrant New Orleans chicory coffee, a copy of the *Times Picayune* and a fresh rose. The hotel provides sodas, coffee, mixers and ice all day long, and tea is served every afternoon.

The Maison de Ville serves neither lunch nor dinner; however, many of the most famous New Orleans restaurants, such as Antoine's, Galatoire's and Brennan's, are all within easy walking distance. When guests return to the hotel after dining out, they will find that their bed has been turned down and a small piece of chocolate, wrapped in foil, has been gently placed on the pillow.

The owners of the Maison de Ville are two New Orleans businessmen, Cornelius White and Terence Hall. The manager is William Prentiss, an experienced hotelier who once worked for the august Hotel Pierre in New York. The three men have developed a simple goal for their establishment: "We want the Maison de Ville to be the best small hotel in the world." It may very well be just that.

THE INNS

Even an institution as timeless as a country inn is changeable. Ownerships are transferred, rooms are redecorated and chefs come and go. Undoubtedly some changes will be made in the establishments written about here. But their general character and appeal will most likely remain intact. In spite of changes, or perhaps because of them, most of these inns have already stood the test of time. Most changeable of all are rates, of course, but current rates are given so that readers will have a clear idea of the range of expense for each establishment. Reservations are necessary for accommodations at all the inns. Maps are provided only for those inns the editors felt particularly hard to locate. In regard to children and pets, it is best to ask each inn specifically about its policy.

BLACK BASS HOTEL, Route 32, Lumberville, Pennsylvania 18933; (215) 297-5770, Herb Ward, Innkeeper. A 6-room inn on the Delaware River. Open all year. Double occupancy rate is $35; $75 for the 2-bedroom and living room suite, including Continental breakfast. Private and shared baths. Restaurant serves lunch and dinner. American Express, Master Charge and Diner's Club credit cards accepted.

DIRECTIONS: Located 8 miles north of New Hope on River Road (Pa. 32).

CHALET SUZANNE, P.O. Drawer AC, Lake Wales, Florida 33853; (813) 676-1477, Carl and Vita Hinshaw, Innkeepers. A 30-room inn consisting of a series of small buildings on the shore of a private lake. Open all year. Double occupancy rates range from $26 to $36; suites, $50. Restaurant serves breakfast, lunch and dinner. From June to October restaurant closed Mondays. All major credit cards accepted. Swimming pool.

DIRECTIONS: 40 miles from Disney World, off Fla. 27, halfway between Cypress Gardens and the Bok Singing Tower. Watch for signs. Inn is located on Fla. 17A, 4 miles north of Lake Wales.

CLIFF PARK INN, Milford, Pennsylvania 18337; (717) 296-6491, Harry W. Buchanan, Innkeeper. A summer hotel in the foothills of the Pocono Mountains. Open from Memorial Day weekend to November. Rates available on request, and include three meals and a day's greens fees. They tend to range from $38 per person per day to $203 for seven days. No credit cards accepted. Private golf course.

DIRECTIONS: Located 1½ miles northwest of Milford off Pa. 6. Watch for signs to inn.

COUNTRY INN, 207 South Washington Street, Berkeley Springs, West Virginia 25411; (304) 258-2210, Jack and Adele Barker, Innkeepers. A 37-room inn located next to the Berkeley Mineral Springs State Park. Open all year. Single occupancy rates range from $16 to $20; double, $19 to $27. Rooms with two double beds range from $30 to $39, depending on occupancy. Suites range from $35 to $44. Restaurant serves breakfast, lunch and dinner. American Express, Master Charge and Visa credit cards accepted.

DIRECTIONS: The inn is located on W.V. 522, adjacent to the state park.

GREYFIELD INN, P.O. Box 878, Fernandina, Florida 32034; (912) 496-7503, Eugene and Essie Horne, Innkeepers. An 8-room inn with 2 cottages, located on Cumberland Island, Georgia. Open all year. Private and shared baths. Rates are $50 per day per person, including all meals, which are served buffet-style from the kitchen. No credit cards accepted.

DIRECTIONS: Greyfield is located on Cumberland Island, and accessible only by private airplane or by Park Service boats from St. Mary's, Ga. and Fernandina Beach, Fla.

L'HOSTELLERIE BRESSANE, P.O. Box 286, Hillsdale, New York 12529; (518) 325-3412, Jean Morel, Innkeeper. A 4-room inn, with an internationally famous restaurant, on the Hudson River. Closed February and March. Room rates are $18 for single or double occupancy with Continental breakfast. Shared baths. Restaurant serves lunch and dinner. All major credit cards are accepted.

DIRECTIONS: Located at the intersection of N.Y. 22 and N.Y. 23, on the east side of the Hudson River, 125 miles north of New York City.

LAMOTHE HOUSE, 621 Esplanade Avenue, New Orleans, Louisiana 70116; (504) 947-1161, Mrs. Gertrude Munson and Mrs. Mimi Munson Langguth, Innkeepers. A 14-room inn on the fringe of the French Quarter, near the Mississippi. Closed from mid-July to August. Double occupancy rates range from $33 to $35; suites, $43; both including Continental breakfast. American Express, Master Charge and Visa credit cards accepted.

DIRECTIONS: Located close to the intersection of Esplanade Avenue and Bourbon Street.

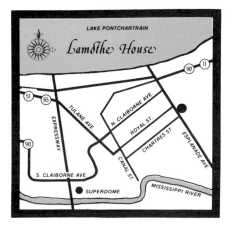

THE MAINSTAY, 635 Columbia Avenue, Cape May, New Jersey 08204; (609) 884-8690, Tom and Sue Carroll, Innkeepers. A 10-room inn located 2½ blocks from the ocean. Closed from December through February. Double occupancy rates range from $25 to $32, including full breakfast and afternoon tea. Private and shared baths. No credit cards accepted.

DIRECTIONS: The inn is located in the center of town, just 2 blocks from Convention Hall.

MAISON DE VILLE, 727 Toulouse Street, New Orleans, Louisiana 70130; (504) 561-5858, William Prentiss, Innkeeper. A small city hotel in the heart of the French Quarter. Open all year. Double occupancy rates range from $65 to $75; suites, $110; cottages from $120 to $185. All rates include Continental breakfast. No credit cards accepted. Swimming pool at the cottages.

DIRECTIONS: Located just off Bourbon Street in the French Quarter.

NU-WRAY INN, Burnsville, North Carolina 28714; (704) 682-2329, Rush Wray and Mrs. Annie Wray Bennett, Innkeepers. A 35-room inn located on the town square. Open all year, but the kitchen may be closed from January through March. Single occupancy rates range from $12 to $15; double occupancy, $20 to $30, with baths. Other rooms with shared baths. Restaurant serves breakfast and dinner, Sunday luncheon. Weekly rates, including all meals, are available by prior arrangement. No credit cards accepted.

DIRECTIONS: Approximately 38 miles north of Asheville, the inn is located in the center of town, on the square.

OLD DROVER'S INN, Dover Plains, New York 12522; (914) 832-9311, Travis Harris, Innkeeper. A 3-room inn midway between New York City and the Berkshires. Closed Tuesdays and Wednesdays, and for three weeks in December. Double occupancy rates range from $50 to $70. Restaurant serves breakfast (to inn guests only), lunch and dinner. No credit cards accepted.

DIRECTIONS: Located on Old Drover's Road, off N.Y. 22, 4 miles north of Wingdale.

THE INN AT PHILLIPS MILL, North River Road, New Hope, Pennsylvania 18938; (215) 862-9919, Brooks and Joyce Kaufman, Innkeepers. The 5-room inn is located on the Delaware River. Open all year, but the restaurant closes in January. Double occupancy rates range from $28 to $38. Restaurant serves breakfast, lunch and dinner. No credit cards accepted.

DIRECTIONS: The inn is located 1½ miles north of New Hope on Pa. 32 (North River Road).

PUMP HOUSE INN, Canadensis, Pennsylvania 18325; (717) 595-7501, H. Todd Drucquer, Innkeeper. An intimate, 4-room inn in the Pocono Mountains. Closed over Christmas from Dec. 10 to 27. Closed Mondays from June 16 to October 16. Closed Mondays and Tuesdays rest of year. Double occupancy rates range from $28 to $36, including Continental breakfast. Restaurant serves lunch and dinner. American Express, Master Charge and Visa credit cards accepted.

DIRECTIONS: Located on Pa. 390, 1½ miles north of Canadensis.

RED FOX TAVERN, Washington Street, Middleburg, Virginia 22117; (703) 687-6301, Nancy Brown Reuter, Innkeeper. A 6-room inn in the Virginia foxhunting country. Open all year. Double occupancy rates range from $30 to $45; $55 for a suite. Restaurant serves lunch and dinner. Breakfast available. Most major credit cards accepted.

DIRECTIONS: Located about 45 miles from downtown Washington, the inn is in the center of Middleburg, on Va. 50.

ROD AND GUN LODGE, P.O. Drawer G, Everglades City, Florida 33929; (813) 695-2101, Martin Bowen, Innkeeper. A 12-room inn located near Everglades National Park. Open all year. Double occupancy rates range from $24 to $28. Restaurant serves breakfast, lunch and dinner. No credit cards accepted. Fishing.

DIRECTIONS: The inn is located on Hibiscus Street, two blocks from the main street of Everglades City, on the Barron River.

ROBERT MORRIS INN, Oxford, Maryland 21654; (301) 226-5111, Kenneth and Wendy Gibson, Innkeepers. A 31-room inn with 1 cottage on the Tred Avon River. Open all year except Christmas day. Single and double occupancy rates are the same and range from $20 to $60; some private baths, most shared. The rate for the cottage, which accommodates 5, is $56. An apartment for 5 is available at $60. Restaurant serves breakfast, lunch and dinner. American Express, Master Charge and Visa charge cards accepted.

DIRECTIONS: From Easton, follow Md. 333 to the end, about six miles. The inn is on the right.

ROYCROFT INN, 40 South Grove Street, East Aurora, New York 14052; (716) 652-9030, Frank and Kitty Turgeon, Innkeepers. The complex includes guest accommodations, craft workshops, restaurant and shop. Open all year. Double occupancy rates range from $28 to $36. Restaurant serves breakfast, lunch and dinner. American Express, Master Charge and Visa credit cards accepted.

DIRECTIONS: Approximately 12 miles east of Buffalo, the inn is located off Main Street, near the Town Hall.

1770 HOUSE, 143 Main Street, East Hampton, New York 11937; (516) 324-1770, Sidney and Miriam Perle, Innkeepers. A 6-room inn located in a Long Island resort town. Open all year. Restaurant open on weekends only during the winter. Single occupancy rates range from $30 to $35; double occupancy, $40 to $55, including Continental breakfast. Restaurant serves lunch and dinner; Taproom serves food after the theater during the summer. Major credit cards are accepted.

DIRECTIONS: N.Y. 27 to East Hampton on Long Island. The inn is located just beyond the village green, on the left, beyond the cupola-topped Clinton Museum.

SWORDGATE INN, 111 Tradd Street, Charleston, South Carolina 29401; (803) 723-8518, Kerry Anderson, Innkeeper. A 5-room inn located in the heart of Charleston's historic district. Open all year. Single occupancy rate is $38; $44 for a double, including breakfast. No credit cards accepted.

DIRECTIONS: Follow the signs to Rutledge Ave. and turn left at Tradd Street. The inn is four blocks down on the right.

WAYSIDE INN, Middletown, Virginia 22645; (703) 869-1797, Bill Castro, Innkeeper. A 21-room inn located in the Shenandoah Valley. Open all year. Double occupancy rates are $26 for a double room, $34 for a suite. Restaurant serves breakfast, lunch and dinner. American Express, Master Charge and Visa charge cards accepted.

DIRECTIONS: Located on Va. 11, twelve miles south of Winchester, in the center of Middletown.

Photograph on page one taken at the Black Bass Hotel by George W. Gardner

Frontispiece photograph taken at the Robert Morris Inn by George W. Gardner

Title page photograph taken at 1770 House by Lilo Raymond

A ROBERT REID, WIESER AND WIESER PRODUCTION CREATED FOR THE KNAPP PRESS, LOS ANGELES
WITH THE EDITORS OF ARCHITECTURAL DIGEST
EDITORIAL ASSOCIATES: GEORGE ALLEN AND TRACY ECCLESINE
DESIGNED AND PRODUCED BY THE VINJE, REID DESIGN STUDIO
COLOR SEPARATIONS BY OFFSET SEPARATIONS CORP, NEW YORK
TYPESET BY THE MONOTYPE COMPOSITION COMPANY, BALTIMORE
BOUND BY THE BOOK PRESS, BRATTLEBORO, VERMONT